The Awakening

Conquering The Sleeping Giant Within

By

Reginald G. Johnson, Ph.D.

To Debbie
A true Spiritual
Warrior
Rosso

ISBN: 1-4107-2979-6 (e-book)
ISBN: 1-4107-2980-X (Paperback)

This book is printed on acid free paper.

1stBooks - rev. 10/28/03

TABLE OF CONTENTS

This is the final stage of your being—where you are "aware" and "awake" to your higher sensory perception and spiritual self. You can now assist others to create love, spiritual advancement and power in their lives, creating the force known as...the Awakening.—

1.

Psychic Ability or Mystical Experience?

The transcendent experience has been scientifically recorded for years and is practiced by humans. We have many names for it and each person is affected by another person's consciousness here on earth and beyond the veil of life.

The term "psychic" has been taken so far out of context, and has become so blemished, it is nearly impossible to believe we will ever have a spiritual "homecoming" to the English language in lookiing for meaning for this term. A psychic is one who uses God-given powers of the Spirit and is usually in an altered and/or controlled state of "pure mental activity" at a very high level; however, a mystic or prophet is usually endowed with another state of being which is "purely intuitive" and which is above and beyond the psychic level—on the dynamic spiritual level. As I have said many times to clients, "Prayer is when *you speak with God*; intuition is *God answering you*."

There are different varieties of "psychic gifts" available to us at times. One is clairvoyance (to see with the mind's eye). God gives you inner vision today, just as He did with the prophets of old. Check out the Bible when Paul said, "Yet when I am among mature Christians, I do speak with words of great wisdom, but not the kind that comes from here on earth, and not the kind that appeals to great men of this world, who are doomed to fall." (I Corinthians 2:6). To some others God gave the gift of clairaudience (clear spiritual hearing)—such was the gift Joan of Arc had. These people hear the voice of God and receive information from a higher plane of existence. Still others are touched with the gift of Psychometry, or dermo-optics, the ability to touch objects and receive accurate information about the owner, whether living or passed on. There are many other gifts as well. This is only to demonstrate that we cannot limit God with our religious beliefs, especially when all religion is man-made. What is more important—your religion or your relationship with God?

Dramatic progress has been made in scientific research into the mind, augmenting our understanding of psychic energy, including both the right and left sides of the brain and their functions, bio-magnetic energy used by "faith healers" of the past for creating "miracles," and the phantom or whole-leaf effect, using Kirlian photography to see "auras" or the life force around all living things.

I grew up Methodist, and was told what was good, bad and ugly—which made me very thirsty for more of the close cosmic experience with God. One should never tell a fresh, young and fertile mind "never" do something—it makes him or her more curious! I read the Bible, participated in the sacrament and other processes and rituals. The church seemed "empty" in providing me with any ways to quench my thirst for knowledge and power from the spiritual standpoint of self-unfolding in the mystical experience. I read stories of Jesus saying that we were sons and daughters of God and that He would provide for our needs—spiritual and physical. Yet, if we saw someone who was spiritually advanced with remarkable mystical skill, we would label them a demon or a fake. Where was the excitement and child-like fun in serving God in my church? God has sent His Spirit, but the "occult" or deeper secrets of God have been mysteriously replaced with robotic programming from the pulpit to the ever-hungry masses seeking true enlightenment.

What human nature does not understand, it seeks to resist or destroy. Who are we to judge the fresh, new messages coming from the heart of God to His children who have open minds and are `willing to hear` that voice today? What would we do with a modern Noah who purportedly "heard" the voice of God?

Everything that `negatively` influences our psychic or soul energy diminishes our very being, and vice versa. When you "posit" or affirm the positive, or change your thinking, other people can "sense" it and are thereby attracted to you; at the same time, your strength is increased.

Your bio-energy is always present in your physical body, as is your spirit. It is your "magnetism" or body electricity that enables the communication between the brain and the other parts of the body. Psychic energy connects you with your own body, other people (and their spirits), as well as to the Universe or God.

When your own energy of the spirit is depleted, it negatively influences your physical body and its strength, making it more susceptible to disease and other ailments. If your body needs nutrients for normal functioning, think how much more your spirit needs the nurturing of prayer, reflection, meditation and ritual to keep it alive!

Your energy, like your "soul," was created in the mind of God many eons ago. In fact, if science (particularly physics) stipulates that matter cannot be destroyed, but only changed, you have been here on this planet many times before. You can even connect with your ancient past or "past lives" when skilled hypnotists regress you using hypnosis.

Ancient cultures and civilizations around the world believe in reincarnation. My first awareness of reincarnation, believe it or not, came from reading the New Testament of the Bible—an unlikely experience according to many Christians who do not believe in it. In Matthew, 11:13- 14; 16:13, Jesus is asking His disciples the following: "*Whom do men say that I, the son of man, am?* "(Matt. 16:13) and the disciples answer

4

"Some say that thou art John the Baptist, some Elias and others Jeremiah or one of the prophets." How could Jesus be any of these other illumined individuals, except by having a previous life? Elias lived hundreds of years before and so did Jeremiah. The fact that Jesus asked the question shows his awareness of the doctrine of reincarnation.

The only contemporary evidence substantiating past lives comes through past life regressions under hypnosis. No matter what our beliefs are, the development of the Christ consciousness is eternal. I don't believe one lifetime is enough time to prepare you for attaining your ultimate spiritual goals to become "Christlike"; in order for these and "greater works" to occur you must be born again many times to learn the different lessons in life, until you become "perfect" as Christ was "perfect." Jesus "…knew the thoughts of men" Matt.12:25. Was this mere psychic energy or a mystical experience? Jesus renamed each of the disciples. He knew who they were in their previous incarnation. Jesus used intuition and not mere "hunches" because he knew when healing occurred, felt virtue leave his body, materialized coins, walked through a wall, spoke to the dead to arise, levitated before eye-witnesses, and again, defied the laws of gravity with his body by walking on water. There were also many prophets, saints and holy men thousands of years before Jesus who demonstrated the great miraculous powers of mind and spirit. Why, then, condemn (true) psychics and mystics?

Many well-meaning believers amaze me with double-mindedness. There are many television evangelists that I listen to in the morning, many of whom quote the words of Christ with authority, telling us we need to "be like Jesus." But when there are those who demonstrate and "do these things and greater works" such as walking on water, changing water into wine, healing the sick, raising the dead, making spit balls on the ground and causing the blind to see, the TV preachers would run out of the church or label the true believer as demonic.

John the Baptist was asked whether he was the incarnation of Elijah or of one of the prophets, to which he replied he did not know. He was "a voice in the wilderness" John.1:21. Jesus knew who John the Baptist was and declared that he was more than a prophet— he was Elijah reincarnated. God spoke His cosmic laws into existence, and they still apply right now, and always will. Great artists, singers, scientists, engineers and others have tapped into the spiritual superhighway for centuries before the Internet. We are motivated by a Power stronger than we are and it is planted in our subconscious mind. If you went to a club where no liquor or wine was sold, and someone arrived at the party and changed the club soda and water into wine before you and other eyewitnesses, what would your reaction be? Jesus used the powers of mind and spirit and said we must do the same, to literally condense time and physical laws in order to effect miraculous change.

My wife's father was very ill from an accident and slipped into a coma. Doctors at the hospital in Burbank, California indicated he had "lost brain mass" and would not be the same in terms of cognitive abilities; he would in fact, they said, be more akin to "a vegetable," and death was imminent. I immediately thought about a Bible scripture, Ecclesiastes 2:12-14, "I saw that wisdom is better than folly, just as light is better than darkness." Light is in the Universe and individualized in your own spirit. I called on the "Light" of the healing angel Raphael, to surround and protect Mr. Morris. I then, spiritually "saw" these incredible circles of light in my mind's eye. I "felt" he was perfect, just as God made him. The "light" penetrated my very being and I "knew" he was healed. Period. The doctors at the hospital called our house very excited looking for my wife, Cynthia, saying they had witnessed "a miracle." I appealed to the Doctor who made all doctors. I believe that the greatest surgeon on earth can perform a healing on the body, but he must wait for the Higher Doctor of the Universe to do the actual healing. Push your powers of mind to the edge. The invisible photons of light which travel at 186,000 miles per second entered that hospital room, became personified and in that light, the dying man was healed.

You are an heir of the family of God—just as the Christ. He said so throughout the Scriptures. We are confined to the limits of the physical body. But your powers of mind are not. A man's body can be jailed for a crime. That same man can use his mind and write a bestseller! When you are led by your heart and not your condition, anything is possible.

I have many clients, and as an Intuitive (or Prophet, or Mystic)—whatever "title" you choose—I am spirit first. People sometimes look up to me as someone with incredible magical powers. The only magic I possess is my faith in God as the Ultimate Reality and Power. The mystical experience comes along when you place your trust, without any questions or without vacillating, in that Power. Each of us has the responsibility to go inside in meditation; to go into the "silence" of that place within and communicate with God. When you go to that place, that is where you behold the reality of God—the mystery of God. Find your spiritual truth. Your religion has nothing to do with "your truth" or the reason that you were born or your sacred contract with God before coming through the mother. Your vehicle on this three-dimensional planet is different from every other person on earth. When you learn to seek and find the "Kingdom within," believe me, you will have a major homecoming with the Divine Reality of your Higher Self, or Christ Consciousness, and it will transform your life forever. Your understanding of what God is to you—whether God,

Goddess, Ascended Masters, or otherwise named—will be the God of your understanding because it will be a loving, profound and elegant one.

Let it be your choice if you are having a psychic experience or a mystical one. Because it is what it is. You learn to experience something deeper than the five senses. Mystics have learned since thousands of years ago that you can inspire, heal, help to transform others and empower them just with your presence.

The fastest way to develop your own ability is through meditation. Meditation is nothing unique or fancy. Meditation is the art of taming the thoughts and focusing the mind on an intent, and the intent is your Divine connection with God. I say the word "God" to cover all the other manifestations and beliefs about God.

What happens with meditation is that you gain an incredible amount of development, and the more you practice, the more profound it is. I suggest fifteen minutes a day, preferably in the morning so that you can wake up with "an attitude of gratitude to increase your spiritual latitude." That is what I tell my students all the time, because you must be grateful for a brand new day, under a newly created sky, made just for you to give thanks. The more thanks you give, the greater your chances of success from the positive flow of life's blessings to you. Anything that you do to focus your attention on calming and centering yourself and tuning in to the Higher Forces and energies is considered meditation. I perform many guided meditations with incredible results.

The kingdom that you are seeking is also seeking you. As a matter of fact it is inside of you.

A fear is a negative wish! A fear, like doubt, is prayer in reverse.

Reginald G. Johnson, Ph.D

2.

Spiritual Self-Defense

Electromagnetic energy is the force field around everyone. These complex structures or "auras" can be affected by people who maintain a negative thought atmosphere such as depression, suicide, etc., and can be directed toward us. These "energy vampires" can be stopped with this exercise in spiritual self-defense.

Everything on this planet and beyond has an electromagnetic energy field called an aura. Although a sofa shipped from a furniture company has an aura, it may appear inanimate or gray-colored, compared to the energy emanated from a plant or a human, which is different in color. When you visit a psychic, he or she is reading the information contained in the aura that carries information about a person, place or thing. Yes, even buildings carry both psychic and "emotional" scarring, which is sometimes mistaken as a "haunting" or ghost energy left by those who were greatly unhappy, depressed or suicidal, or afflicted with any other negative thought formations; these create negative vibratory fields in homes and buildings. The past, present and future can be "read" from all things.

When someone attempts to control you, they attempt to "invade" your sacred space and you can definitely feel it. If it feels uncomfortable to you, you think you don't like the person for some odd reason. This is usually because their intentions may not be the best for you. These "psychic vampires," or energy-draining individuals, want something from you—love, friendship, money, sex, your good energy, or whatever. There is noting wrong with another's energy if that energy is good. But for optimal health on all levels of your being, everyone should keep their own energy in their "own space."

Remember that you are spirit first and then the person you are named. You will always be spirit. Therefore, you have the attributes and qualities of God, who fashioned you into being. Therefore, rejoice in your uniqueness and value to God. Psychic attacks don't occur as often as people want to believe. However, if your space is invaded, imagine a glowing white light around your body, shaped like an egg which protects every part of your body. Sense this protective layer with your feeling nature and ask God (or the God of your understanding) to empower you at this moment with protection. This will strengthen the light. Know that nothing can penetrate this shield. Also know that every positive thought and feeling either neutralizes or destroys negative thoughts and feelings. Give a whispered prayer of thanks. You are a part of Divinity animated by God-force and you will always exist. Know that your thoughts are directed in love and away from anxiety, and indecision. Open your mind always to be a receptive channel for God, because you already are. You are the offspring of GOD! Say that to yourself each morning at least 10 times while taking in your breath of thanksgiving for a new day under a new sky. Watch your results. They are error proof.

Your central being becomes centered and fear will vanish. When you trust in your Higher Self, or God Self, that is the secret universal key to rest, revitalization and longevity.

ginald G. Johnson, Ph.D

Faith transcends the divisions of time and space, bending physical reality into the reality prayed for.

Reginald G. Johnson, Ph.D

3.

Expanding Your Power

Consciousness is energy which can be expanded by individuals, including you! Learn to increase your awareness and power, and to maintain spiritual, mental, and physical balance by taking charge of your psychic awareness and abilities.

We want to expand our power and consciousness. Everyone speaks of consciousness. But what is it? The best way, I believe, to define consciousness is: *an inner awareness given to us at birth that is ageless, powerful and eternal, represented as a unit of cosmic perception of our higher selves, as a reminder of our God selves.*

When you have a local perception of something, you "know" that it is here or there because you are seeing it, hearing it, tasting it, touching it or smelling it. But then there is a nonlocalized perception. It is beyond time, space and physically perceptual reality. We are capable of that perception and our eternality with the Unseen. We have an evidence of awareness that is never separate from us and is always with us, and in fact, is "in" us and "is" us. We are never separate from God.

Therefore, perception allows us to have an awareness of existence in all of the various forms it assumes to us. In discovering your awakening and expanding your consciousness, it is important to realize that you are never separate from the Source, or God. It is a false statement that God is "out there somewhere." I believe that God is everywhere simultaneously, including in me. That is why it makes sense that your angels or "guides" can be contacted immediately. One of the best ways to expand consciousness is through meditation. In meditation you deliberately draw your attention from all of the outside sources and external conditions around you—including chatter, emotions, and so on—and you localize all of your personal energy to experience "self," realizing that God is in you, expressed as "you" in this moment in time.

When you are fully in a perfect state of meditation for your own human growth and higher consciousness, you learn to find out who you really are. It's pretty amazing—I tell my students all the time that "repetition creates impact" and this is true. Repeat the practice of finding the self by blocking out all the negative influences; and if they are not completely blocked out, you learn how to deal with them as something transitory, almost as something happening outside of yourself. When you are experiencing wholesome living in meditation, you become a calmer person, with intellectual strength and spiritual powers; your awareness is clearer. You are more progressive in your spiritual awakening and your growth is more spontaneous. When you experience spiritual growth—becoming fully awake using not only your intellectual but also your intuitive powers to analyze or discover who you are as your "self" and your relationship with God—something amazing happens. You eliminate fear. It has been said that F.E.A.R. is False Evidence Appearing Real. Your faith in your Higher Good or Higher Self is the only Reality that there is. That is the discovery of expanding your powers and ability in consciousness.

For thousands of years, people in power have always wanted to control those who were not in power. For the sake of power certain principles were intentionally created, such as the concept of Hell and burning forever. Explain how you, as a parent, could go through pain, suffering, and the sacrifice of giving everything to nurture your child, providing loving comfort, clothing, food, shelter, and education to foster their care—and send them to hell forever? Well, it's true, some kids do appear to be the descendents of personified evil with their rebellious behavior and matching tempers; but to release their bodies to everlasting punishment? I remember reading something once that said, "Religion is for those afraid of going to hell, and true spirituality is for those of use who've been there already." I do not mean to make light or fun of anyone's personal beliefs, but many have been misinformed, unfortunately.

In all the religions of the earth, there are many accounts of angels and saints appearing to those of faith, and accounts of healings and other miracles. God is not racist, nor biased. There are many written accounts of children seeing angels throughout history and from every part of the globe! There is a Biblical passage, in the New Testament, where Jesus said he could have called 10,000 angels. If we are to do greater things than He (as Jesus said we would), why not communicate with our angels and guides who have made themselves known to us? Imagine the power you have as a human made in the image and likeness of God. The purpose here is to help you expand your human and spiritual potential and to grow into your highest reality to help and love others—including yourself. As you expand in your own highest light and dimension, you may experience difficulty in loving yourself. Many people get angry with God and have a lot of fear-based misunderstandings and superstitions from times past which need not be repeated in your process of learning the truth.

Focusing on expanding your consciousness through the process of meditation, and specificallyfocusing on each part of your body through guided meditation, helps to improve the circulatory system, effectively lowers blood pressure, decreases the heart rate and gives you a calmer outlook on life. You become more patient, while giving a super charge to the immune system. You have mind-control over your body, especially where pain is concerned. You become more healing in your own nature. When you focus on your emotional self, you have a deeper meaning in your relationships with others and an "inner peace" that is beyond human description. With meditation you feel more motivated in your quest for spiritual development. Creativity, perceptual ability, and clarity is increased tremendously.

You feel closer to God in meditation. Once you get this connection, it is an amazing experience. A feeling of total joy and elation happens. A doctor friend of mine once told me, "Whatever happens to you in this life is not important, but how you deal with it is." Meditation is the vehicle for helping you to "deal with it" on this physical plane. It is your responsibility to meditate every day and usually at the same time. Why meditate at the same time? Because practice is the key. Ritual is the key. Your mind, which is very active, tries to throw what frequent meditators call "monkeys," or active thought patterns, in your way to prevent you from focusing on "stilling" the mind. Your left brain with all of its analytical functions will always try to overpower the right, creative side of the brain in its attempt to help you attain spiritual perfection. Again, with practice, you can achieve mastery over your own mind. It is your own mind that engineered the process for you to arrive here, through time and space, through the mother vehicle (mom) of your choice, to come into this three-dimensional plane, the school planet called Earth.

If you are the loner type, you may want to experience meditation in the solitude and sacred space of your own home. If you like to be around others to explore meditation, to have the reinforcement of the physical presence and mind power of others, you may want to get with a group. In my basic meditation and psychic development classes, the students give details of their meditations—every feeling, scene, color, physical touch on the body, temperature changes, and what they "saw" in their minds. After giving me information about their specific meditation experience, I am then able to interpret the higher emotional, spiritual and physical issues currently experienced in life. If you are going to do meditation alone, it is recommended that you keep a journal. Just as important is a dream journal, even when you think you don't remember your dreams. Your Higher Self may be communicating with you in the dream state.

Before any meditation exercise, I always balance the energy fields in the room, or "clear" the energy with a special prayer to acknowledge God, since meditation is a spiritual practice.

Sometimes I call on the special angels of Earth, Air, Fire and Water. (These may be called different things in different religious practices, such as The Quarters, or The Watchtowers) These are the elements things are made of on this planet.

When I perform that prayer, those attuned to that vibration can actually see and feel a dramatic energy change in the room. A woman attending my monthly New Moon Rituals took photographs when I was performing the prayer, and when the photographs were developed; there were four distinct, pink-colored, perfectly shaped "orbs" around me. I also appeal to the Holy Spirit; and it really gets exciting at this point, because this is the "prophecy" or psychic prediction and reading phase of the event, which is always positive and powerful.

Keep a positive outlook and open mind during meditation. Like anything else, it takes time and practice. Before you begin your meditation, have a pen and paper handy to jot down notes when your meditation has ended. Do not meditate for a long time in the beginning. Quality is more important here than quantity. In the spiritual realm of reality, there is no time or distance. Therefore, start out with about fifteen minutes in duration; you may increase it later. Breathing is critical while meditating. If you feel uneasy about something, or if your energy is off balance, sometimes when you are meditating very deeply, especially where breathing is concerned, you may find your body "jerking" or "jumping." I call these involuntary movements "angelic confirmation." This means that a lot of the energy coming through the energy field of your own body is too much to handle at once. Take your time. Slow down and get totally focused. You may want to stand up, stretch, loosen the body and get ready before you meditate, and even after you do so, to realign the frequency of your body.

If you are sitting during your meditation, you do not want to cross your legs and arms. Your posture must be perfect enough to allow the energy to flow freely from the top of your body to the soles of the feet. You must breathe psychically—meaning from the diaphragm, deeply, in the beginning—hold it and then exhale. I have instructed my students, during consciousness expansion meditations, to not let anything negative in as we sit in a circle (which is symbolic of binding protection). Then, we take a deep breath in through the nose, andhold it to the mental count of 5-4-3-2-1. At this point, they are instructed to release the air slowly and deliberately out of the mouth in a long stream of air as they relax their neck, back, shoulders, arms, forearms, hands, chest and stomach, thighs and legs, all the way through the toes to the ground, releasing any residual negative energy from any impacting sources. This exercise is repeated a few times until the energy is focused and they are relaxed. Some students are more advanced than others. This does not matter because we all start with cleansing negative energies before starting on our cosmic flight. Additionally, some of my students—and you may, too—experience a "rocking" or "swaying" sensation. If this sensation is followed by or preceded by a strange or disconnected feeling, do not be alarmed. This is the initial process of leaving your body through soul travel. This is why it is imp

synchronize your breathing and awareness in your ph

body as you relax, to eliminate all fear. And this is the oth

reason it is important to cover yourself with white light and/or

prayer before and after meditation. Do not get caught up into

physical phenomena immediately. This pitfall reminds me of the

prayer, *"Dear God, please grant me patience. And hurry up!"* That is an unrealistic prayer. You should not

ask for patience, growth and enlightenment in the same manner

as you warm up a slice of pizza in the microwave, expecting

instant results. It takes experience. Your body, mind and

emotions are all going through a physical, mentative and astral

change, which does not evolve overnight.

Now we know that consciousness is energy and that it is

more powerful than electricity or atomic energy—it is the

energy that creates life, goes beyond physical death and

contacts those who have "crossed over." This is the

consciousness that can affect another person's consciousness

beyond the physical earth-bound limits of time and space. You

are a unit of God consciousness and therefore possess God

consciousness. Mystics, psychics, occultists, spiritual advisors,

and ancient seers from the past have always astounded us with

their ability, and so can you—you can make miracles happen in

your life on purpose. Your income, popularity, impossible or

instant healings all happen because you were born to enlighten

quality of life on earth, for others as well

⋮ in expanding consciousness. You may
tape and play it each night at the same
time, to create your sacred space in evolving spiritually to the
next level. You will protect yourself from psychic attack and
people will respond accordingly, including those who have no
physical body. Tape record the following: "Relax. I take
a deep breath in through my nose, holding it,
counting backwards to five—four—three—two—
one. As I exhale the energy out of my mouth
very slowly in a stream of air, I relax my
neck, back, shoulders, chest, stomach, arms,
forearms, fingers, buttocks, thighs, legs and
toes—I release all energy from the day which
may have caused me stress. Again, as I breathe
in deeply and hold my breath, I release it
backwards on the count of five—four—three—
two—one, repeating the process of letting go
and relaxing each part of my body—my neck,
back, shoulders, chest, stomach, arms,
forearms, fingers, buttocks, thighs, legs and
toes. I totally let go of tension. I will
imagine in this space that a beautiful, white
Light as radiant as white sunlight with the
feeling of electric white milk, blankets my
entire body; tingling, vibrating and protecting
me and shielding me with comfort and against

outside forces. This energy of white Light shields me with a mother's love. As I take another deep breath, I see a very still, blue sky without a cloud in it. I am now on the white sands of a beach where a cruise ship floats in the distance as I relax in the sun's rays of warmth as it tingles my body in the beach chair where I sit. My breathing is normal and I am aware of the relaxing feeling I am having. As I slowly get up from my chair, I walk toward the water. As I look down into the incredible blue aquamarine colors, I see a school of multi-colored, exotic fish playing and swimming, having fun. As I get up from the chair, feeling the warm sand under my feet, I am seeing before me in the immediate distance, a man whose face is not clearly defined, but he seems to be bright in appearance, almost luminous. I also sense a tremendous amount of love from him. He instructs me with his mind, to use my index finger and write the first names of any person who needs forgiveness from me, in the sand. As I write the name, or names of these people, he smiles at me. As I look down at the names in the sand, he stretches his hand toward the ocean and a beautiful wave comes in washing away the names, leaving only white foam from the water and it too, recedes to the ocean. He lets me know mentally that everything is forgiven of all parties involved, as the names go into the watery grave of the ocean's forgiving depths of love and eternity. As I look up to thank him, he is no longer there, and a sense of compassion is all over me. I relax my body, and awaken refreshed with a renewed sense of power and love from this consciousness expansion and forgiveness exercise."

What did you think about the exercise? Did you have any sensations, or did you stay in a restful, sleepy state? Did you fall asleep? Whatever your experience, write it down here.

_____

_____

_____

_____

Remember to keep a meditation journal. When you learn to do this often and more vividly, seeing the pictures as real, you are on your way and your path is carved to experiencing miracles in your life—literally! Some students in my class, when counting backwards, felt peaceful, but some felt a sense of falling backwards, or going down. Some students clearly pictured the sand, the beach, the ocean and the fish. Others felt that the figure of the man who appeared on the beach was either a spirit guide, an angel, or Jesus. These energies are just as real as we are! Some students felt nothing except "safety."

No matter how advanced you are in your abilities, you may "sense" or "feel" things or even "hear" ocean waves. Every gift is different. When you "see" in your mind's eye the details with clarity, it signals that you are on your way. Keep practicing and never give up!

Again, do the exercises each day. Repeating them in this way, it will happen so easily for you, you will go through the meditations not realizing how profound your experience was until later. You will be releasing stress, building self-esteem and confidence, and lowering your blood pressure. Does this sound like a vengeful voodoo practice, negative magic or some supernatural dark practice? This is merely a simple matter of the human body's ability to relax, unclutter the mind, and focus on the clarity and intent of your accomplishment. Remember to always approach your meditation with a positive attitude, without tension, anger, fear, resentment, anxiety, or other negative emotions causing stress. Enter the "kingdom within" with positive energy. If you need peripheral devices such as incense, or to burn small pieces of sage to clear the room of negative energy, do so. You may use an oil burner to emit wonderful fragrances such as lavender and patchouli oil to get into the "mood" of meditation. The number-one emotion to take to the inner sanctum is love. When you do, even those who may have felt sick will walk into your sacred space and feel

It will give the body a boost and help the immune oducing healing body chemicals!

This is a meditation I find soothing and very profound. You should tape record this meditation as well so that you can always replay it in your sacred space that you have recorded. Here goes: "First, I am going to relax. As I take a deep breath in through my nose, I will hold it for the mental count of five—four—three—two—one, releasing, as I exhale through my mouth, relaxing my neck, back, shoulders, chest, stomach, arms, forearms, fingers, buttocks, thighs, legs and toes—I release all energy from the day which may have caused me stress. Again, as I breathe in deeply and hold my breath, I release it backwards on the count of five—four—three—two—one, repeating the process of letting go and relaxing each part of my body—my neck, back, shoulders, chest, stomach, arms, forearms, fingers, buttocks, thighs, legs and toes. I totally let go of tension freely into the Universe where it will be recycled properly. There is a beautiful and Divine Light of God's sacred energy protecting me and surrounding my body. Every atom of my body is protected by the force of God's love, shielding me and engulfing me with comfort and safety. This energy shield was with me at birth. This sacred and holy energy is my life *force and Higher Sensory Perception that I was endowed with. I now approach and see a beautiful field of the greenest grass I have ever seen; there are spectacular purple-colored, snowcapped mountains in the background; beautiful pine trees freshen the air with an incredible fragrance, mixed with floral essence. I will now rest on the grass for a moment. I have the sensation now that I can float, defying the physical laws of gravity. As I do so, I sense myself slowly rising from the grass, looking down below me. I see the incredible panorama of grass, birds and mountains as I float upwards. I notice I am standing at the top of the mountain where I can comfortably meditate. I note an overwhelming feeling of love. This feeling is familiar because I sense an incredible Presence of an angel Guide. This illumined energy is someone I am being reacquainted with, and there is nothing but love and warmth from this Person. I feel warmth, protection and security from this Being. This Being has been with me since I decided to come to earth. This Presence of love and power reaches out to me and gently taps me on my forehead. I feel an electric surge of power go through my body—cleansing, healing, expanding my intuitive ability and taking me to another level of consciousness. I feel soothing energy from the top of my scalp to the soles of my feet. There is a circling motion around my body, empowering and aligning me with the frequencies of the Godhead from which I came. As I feel this beautiful sensation, my body now floats downward alongside the mountain, going back to the grass—floating magically, swiftly and safely back to this beautiful, lush green grass that is comforting, soft and fragrant. As I lay here, I am still and happy remembering everything that has happened. At the count of ten, I will be totally refreshed, fully awakened, and will journal this information in my meditation notebook—ten—nine—coming up— eight—coming up higher—seven—feeling good-- six—comfortably relaxed—five—coming up higher and feeling better—four—three— ascending and feeling very good—two—the energy is charged in my face—and one—the energy is on the top of my head; every part of my body is fully awake and conscious.* Journal this information, sensing and taking note of everything such as:

What did you feel?_____

Did you smell the pine and other fragrances?_____

Did you "see" the energy Being of love? _____

Was it familiar to you?_____Other

notations:_____

We maintain a journal because we are immortal, spiritual beings having this human experience, which should be joyful and tranquil. You are "getting dream impressions" and in many cases, *answers* to probing questions. When you are in a state of stillness and silence, although you sleep, those messages from your angels and guides will help to "awaken" you to your own self-awareness, spiritual and emotional maturity. Revisit your journal or diary often and you will experience the voice of God in your higher self.

Reginald G. Johnson, Ph.D

The kingdom of God is within, "said Jesus. We must go inside ourselves to find our mending of life's broken toys. No one can repair them for us.

Reginald G. Johnson, Ph.D

4.

Attracting the Love Of Your Life

What you think about, you talk about; what you talk about, you manifest—including the love of your life. Find out the ritual for attracting your soul mate.

Many people attract love into their lives with an invisible Help and Power of which they know very little. The "Source" is God. When you think thoughts of love, you create an atmosphere of love to attract itself. You may wish and hope or strategize about the "love of your life" and then make a huge mistake, only to discover this was not the person. That is why it is critically important to attract someone with your mind or "like" spirit. Do you love yourself? Not from the standpoint of conceit—this is about loving yourself by being thankful that you have the inner capacity to love God inside you; and loving your neighbors and blessing others because of your self-love (respect)! Prayer and/or meditation should be a major element of daily life for yourself and for the one you wish to attract as a soul mate.

Look at how open children are to others. They are born with kindness, thoughtfulness, consideration and pure love. How were you "taught" about love? Our children learn by our example. They are taught prejudice, bias, racism and the like—but they become victims because their parents were victims and their parents were victims and so forth, not understanding the power and profundity of God's love for themselves and their ability to attract that in others. Like attracts like.

The Holy Bible says we are made in the "image and likeness" of God, which means that in the power of likeness we can attract to us anything we desire, including the love of our life! Out of everything else on this planet, love is so powerful, it can literally move mountains—the mountains of doubt, the mountains of despair, the mountains of terrorism and hatred, the mountains of war and self-doubt can all be removed. What is a soul mate? The soul mate is the person that you attract to you with all the cosmic elements and familiarity of the mirror of who you want in your life, who you believe you could love forever. This is not necessarily the person you have known in another life—although that does happen for Karmic reasons. But the soul mate is the person you've attracted in your life, with qualities you admire and are familiar with, who knows how to "nurture" a relationship and not "order" one. He or she is attracted to you with your hearts beating and pulsating in the same rhythm, and you know that this person loves you unconditionally as well as themselves. No one in the relationship is a doormat or errand runner in the relationship, but the other is an equal partner with you for the rest of your life. It does not matter cosmically what body that person is in, because when you love someone, you love them unconditionally; and you choose only that person because you are forming not only a physical bond, but a spiritual one. There is an emotional "bonding cord" between you and that person, soul-to-soul, for a lifetime—and if you are fortunate enough, for many lifetimes to come.

How Do We Attract A Soul Mate? Well, Cosmic Intelligence (God) indicates that the first law of the Universe is love. You must love all unconditionally, including yourself. Hate, fear and resentment cost too much on the spiritual plane of reality and prevent evolutionary cosmic growth. You were born a divine, perfect cosmic being and must start to love yourself right where you are, and you will attract love to you—that's the rule. You may attract someone who does not have or meet the physical qualifications you desire—either you can love him or her in spite of that, or attract someone else. The new attraction may be a bit shallow when you stop and realize that you must express love divinely.

You cannot love ONLY based on someone's physical appearance or beauty. The person may be an angel by day and the Antichrist by night. Sometimes you may have to find something to substitute for the physical attributes—where is the intelligence and true love he or she is willing to give? Look for something true and binding to you. God may have brought this person into your life for a reason.

Sometimes you may go through relationships like glasses of water. Are you filled with God's Spirit to attract the love of your life? I believe that you are. You are special and there will never be another "you" in a trillion years in a trillion galaxies. It is important that you learn to raise your vibration, love yourself, and send out love into the Universe, so that when it returns to you, this will be true love. You will experience what I term "cosmological synchronicity." That's a mouthful. When the Holy Spirit affirms and validates the experience you are seeking, you will know that God did this from your treatment, prayer, meditation, or spellcasting—it has all come from your faith. This is the answer. Someone said to me recently, "When you pray, you are talking to God; intuition is God talking back!" Always be alert and aware of that still, small voice "in your head," because that is God answering your request.

Love is everything. The entire world is governed by the power of love. It is the nature of your basic self and makes you spiritually complete. It seeks union with others. The person that you've connected with, the person you love—this is your soulmate, for no matter how many incarnations. In the Bible, the Ten Commandments say we must love God with all our heart, soul and mind; this is the first and greatest commandment, and the second one, according to the Bible, is like the first—that you are to love your neighbor as yourself.

There is a constant search for that love within us. I was listening to my wife, Cyhthia, read aloud the other night to me, from a book she purchased from a metaphysical bookstore about the Holy Spirit. What amazed me were the things the apostle Paul had written. There was a passage that said, "Though I speak with the tongues of men and of angels and have not love, I am become as sounding brass or a tingling cymbal. And, although I have the gift of prophecy and understand all mysteries and all knowledge and though I have all faith so that I could remove mountains and have not love, I am nothing." This is very true. She went on to read about the tenets of love—love is long-suffering, kind, does not envy, does not want, is not "puffed up" (pride); does not behave unseemingly. After listening to her, it reaffirmed my belief that we are never separated from God; therefore, we are never separated from love.

When we look into our own clairvoyance, dreams, and other realms of the invisible, we long for the unity of God's Spirit. If we do not have love, we have fear, which produces hate. They cannot co-exist. True love is simply knowing about the spiritual unity of everything in life. This triggers a thought about the spiritual practice of Wicca—the tenderly positive religion of the earth dedicated to God and Goddess (aspects of God and many facets of the Godhead. Did you think everybody in Heaven was male?) Christianity and Wicca are close in union with each other whether the two belief systems know it or not. I saw a bumper sticker which read, "Christianity has Pagan DNA." I laughed out loud. Their belief: "Respect all life. Respect all things." "Harm Ye None." This is love of everything living created by God, including the earth herself. This fills our souls with love and we, therefore, attract Divine love that much closer to our hearts. When you realize that you and everyone on the planet are "neighbors," you have made the first step toward unfolding and manifesting your immortal self. This makes you feel and become beautifully divine. Your soulmate, with those same properties, will find you through the laws of attraction.

The grandchildren of love—faith, long-suffering, patience, and the rest—create an amazing "inner" experience that brings extraordinary results springing from the inside. You lose criticism and condemnation of other people and things because you will realize you speak against God who made them and God who is "in" them. Love is the guiding and motivating force on the physical plane and spiritual level. Every life, city, school, institution and child is important—and part of the Divine nature and plan of God. You become a walking, talking miracle once you realize that everything and everyone is connected and loving from that standpoint. Loving yourself allows you to love everyone else. Love heals and is medicinal because it heals.

When you trust in love and think about love, all you can receive and attract toward you is just that—Love. It is the one power that rules the Universe.

It is amazing when the Holy Spirit (which the original Hebrew text considers "female") speaks through someone and provides the astute listener with Divine revelation and angelic confirmation. Cynthia and I were on the subject of soulmates one afternoon in great discussion and she mentioned, in her profound and authoritative manner, how one had to love themselves first and know God's love before blindly finding a soulmate. This is truth from the Holy Spirit.

I believe that when we are born into some families, with all of the psychological maladjustments among siblings and other family members, we must seek God to unwind any negative programming, and to prevent permanent emotional and spiritual "scar tissue" from the deprivation of love that may have occurred in our formative years.

You attract to you the vast compendium of all your emotional, spiritual, psychological, sexual and developmental qualities you experience growing up into adulthood. This includes your personality and attitudinal traits as well. However, you may think, "How on earth did I ever attract this nut case into my life?" The real question should be, "Why did I attract this person into my life and what lesson am I to learn from it?" When your thoughts are rightly directed by the power of your spiritual self under Divine guidance, and with application of the love of God, you will know your "soulmate" because it will be verified mystically as all of God's laws are.

In my experience and practice, women are naturally more endowed with intuition and accept it generally more so than men do. I noticed this to be true as well, hearing from radio listeners on various male-dominated programs. There is one station in San Bernardino, California which is alternative rock-based and male-dominant, whose listeners I found to be open to Spirit, yet afraid of "in person" readings. It appears more and more that men are attuning themselves with the energy of God through personal transformation initiated by their female partners. Of course, this is not true in all cases all of the time. The contemporaneous woman is being filled with the Holy Spirit, or Goddess archetype, as was prophesied in the Bible, "In the last days, I will pour out My Spirit." So, listen to those wonderful, beautiful sisters, moms and daughters, because they are sacred in their understanding that God is Love, and with that knowledge will not condemn, damage, destroy or punish anyone.

As offspring of the Divine, we are to comply with the Divine Order of the Holy Counsel to nurture our loving bond with others to balance our own karma. For our eternal journey back to God, eliminating the false sense of self is crucial. We are NEVER separate from God. Learn to "see" God in everyone and your soulmate will appear. God is the only power there is. This is the beginning of your own awareness and psychic maturity. When we stop believing that we need the approval of someone to make us perfect or accepting of ourselves, we are automatically uplifted from the self-imposed slavery of feeling inferior. Your "inner" speech or affirmations of love for God and your own uniqueness, will attract to you those people, or that person, of the same psychic frequency as yours. That person who is most attracted to your frequency and bond is your soulmate.

Every person that you meet is special. They deserve love just as you do. Every person is an expression of God. If you judge that person, you are judging God. Jesus declared, "Do not judge." Learn to look at this person from an intuitive perspective. See them as an angel in progress or "work" in progress. It does not matter if it's your boss, your limo driver (if you're that blessed), mother-in-law, or anyone else. Every person is unique. Learn to look past that part of them that is annoying to you and see their greatness. If you can see love, you can see your soulmate.

In your mind, when you are meditating and are quiet and still, perform your relaxation techniques as outlined earlier in this book with deep breathing and light.

Soulmate Exercise: Imagine what the ideal soulmate would be for you. Try to "see" what you are looking for in this person and be very specific. What are their physical characteristics—what does he or she look like? "See" yourself with this person holding hands; looking into each others' eyes embracing, smiling; feeling joy and having a great time. Create this person in your world and in your thoughts. Do not worry if you cannot see a face. In my meditation class, I say the same thing to my students when they are manifesting their angels into existence for their inner vision. The more specific you are, the more rapidly the "person" will come into your life. Next, I don't want you to be "too" specific, because it does not allow the creativity of the Universe to bring the person into your life—which leaves out the fun. Check your feeling nature. What does it feel like to be with this person emotionally? Ask God (or your idea of Divinity) to bring this person to you. Feel good about seeing the person. Go all the way. For example, if you are single, the next time you are ready for dinner, instead of snacking in front of the TV or eating out, make dinner for yourself at home and make another place at the table for your un-manifested soulmate. Pour a liquid into the glass, and then imagine that the person is there. You would not throw the extra serving of food away, of course; you can always save it for later. But in your mind and in the realm of the spirit, this person already exists. Your ritual is real to your subconscious mind, so that with emotional intent and repetition, it will "create" the impact desired. You are made from a Creator—therefore, you have the "ability" to create. Do this for 30 days. Congratulations on your new soulmate!

Reginald G. Johnson, Ph.D

Ask God to be part of your daily, monthly and yearly life plans. He planned the Universe and laid its foundation; surely He can guide you successfully and lovingly.

Reginald G. Johnson, Ph.D

5.

Attracting Money and Prosperity

Money is energy which begins with the mental consciousness of prosperity. As a child of God, the King of the Universe, we should not be bankrupt— ever! Attract money with a change of awareness.

Money is energy which begins with the mental consciousness of prosperity. As a child of God, the King of the Universe, we should not be bankrupt in any sense—morally, mentally, or spiritually. We attract actual money with a change of awareness.

"I am so broke." "I am so broke I can't even pay attention." "I'll never be wealthy." "Being rich is for other people." These statements may seem trite and trivial to you, but if they are *spoken* by you and fueled with belief and certainty, your subconscious mind will register this information coming from your spirit as "truth" and you will push away money from you as if you are sweeping dirt off the floor with a broom. This is because your thinking is the instrument to attract money. However, all of your thinking must be positive because money is energy.

The vibration of money is energy. Not attracting prosperity, wealth, and longevity to you is an insult of the sacred contract made by you prior to arriving on earth through the vehicle of your mother. You are the royal heir to the Higher Power inside you—so listen to the inner dialogue of your dreams; learn from them and win control over your life! The King of the Universe will never be bankrupt or broke. Change your thinking and change your life. There is no pleasure in pain and no respect in poverty—financial, social, emotional, or spiritual. One statementthat stands out in my mind is from the lips of Christ, who said, "The Kingdom of Heaven is within." If you want something, "seek ye first the kingdom of Heaven and all these things shall be added unto you." Since the Kingdom is within us, we must first go within ourselves to recognize that there is an individualized process of God, Who is never separate from *who we are*. This means that a complete, individualized unit of consciousness as us, representing God, is always wealthy, abundant and lavish right where we are, ready to manifest itself. This "kingdom power" is available to each person born of a woman on this planet. If your heart is truly open to love through stillness and meditation, the limits of lack will be forgotten, *allowing* the free-flowing miraculous power of prosperity to flow through you because of your conscious awareness fueled by your belief and the principles of abundance.

Did you know there are actually angels of prosperity waiting at your door; at your purse, at your wallet—ready to magnify your wealth and abundance? My wife, Cynthia, and I opened an employment agency in the heart of the recession in the 1980's. Talk about faith! However, with the news reports ushering in a "doom and gloom" policy on a daily basis, my wife was considering buying into the world's belief system, which is not the Source of abundance. We both immediately realized that everything is possible with God; and as we are part of the Universe, everything we do, God does with us. This includes the actions in our hearts, thoughts and minds. I reminded my wife that there was an existing client willing to pay us a full agency fee of twenty-two percent of the annual salary, which meant about ten-thousand dollars for us, if we could find someone who could speak fairly good English, typed about one hundred ten words per minute and (although many firms no longer use it) could skillfully use shorthand at about one hundred twenty words per minute. Cynthia said, "Okay, honey. Let's look at the current reality in the refrigerator! This is serious." I appealed to the Universal Loan Officer called God who does not want an interest on any loan. I then said to her, "At approximately three o'clock this afternoon, an applicant will enter our office, without an appointment, which is unusual; and she will fit all the requirements."

At three o'clock that afternoon, my wife sat in the office trying to work things out in consciousness. There was a knock on the door, and one of the counselors opened the door to an attractive girl in her early to mid-twenties. She had blonde hair, was dressed very nicely in what looked like a designer dress neatly fitted to her thin frame. When asked if she had an appointment, she replied "No. I noticed the sign on the door which said *by appointment only*, but I thought since I was in the neighborhood I would take a chance." My wife asked if she typed. She indicated she typed about one hundred and ten words per minute. Cynthia then asked, "Do you use shorthand? I know it's something many of our clients no longer use, but this client needs someone who uses shorthand." The young lady, who had a British accent, assured us she used shorthand at the speed of one hundred twenty words per minute.

Needless to say, we got the paperwork handled and sent her to the client, who was so impressed, they forwarded a check that afternoon by motorcycle courier in the amount of ten thousand dollars. She was hired on the spot and we were happy with the results! The Kingdom of Heaven awaits everyone who is willing to remove the veil of darkness and ignorance because of fear, replacing it with the illuminated truth of faith in God who is *in* us, working *as us*. Closer than your next heartbeat and breath, God is. The power of belief brings about incredible results. When you open your mouth and mind

as gratitude to God, you increase the magnifice.
condition of infinite prosperity individualizing itself in your daily
experience. God is your supply, not your job.

Speaking of jobs, several years ago my wife and I attended
a free presentation which was cleverly disguised as something
else we did not want to attend because we were not interested
in selling detergent, soaps, or household products. However,
the facilitator made an interesting comment about jobs. He
wrote on the blackboard the initials J.O.B. He said this stands
for "Just Over Broke," referring to most job salaries or wages
that are just enough to keep you coming back for more. That
was revelatory to me because it made me more aware of the
ineffable truth that God is the Source of money and all
prosperity. God is male, female; God and Goddess, Infinite
Mind, and anything else you call God, depending on your
personalized truth and belief system. It will be done unto you
according to your belief. You are the master *Self* within. Say
to yourself, *"Prosperity belongs to me. Abundance
belongs to me and is flowing into my life right
now as I say these words."*

Exercise: Get a green candle of any length, take a hair
pin, toothpick, or ink pen, and with your writing, or "power"
hand, inscribe the symbol $ into the horizontal side of the
candle. In addition, inscribe an amount of money that "feels"
comfortable to you in the wax as well. For example, 10K would

mean $10,000. Now take two drops of olive oil or patchouli oil and "anoint" your candle by rubbing the oil directly over the symbol in the wax in an upward motion, representing the male energy of God ("Father Sky"), and on the opposite side of the candle, use two more drops on the candle in a downward stroke, representing the female energy of God ("Mother Earth), so that they are balanced. Some people roll the candle in cinnamon or crushed basil. But that is not necessary. Light the candle, being extra careful and repeat the affirmation above: *"Prosperity belongs to me. Abundance belongs to me and is flowing into my life right now as I say these words."* You should perform this faith-building ritual every day *at the same time* if possible. When you "feel" energy flow through you, end your session with the candle. DO NOT BLOW THE CANDLE OUT! This way you "blow away" your money and prosperity to the wind. Instead, squeeze it out or use a candle snuffer to extinguish the flame safely. Do this on a daily basis and watch money flow into your life. I love this ritual for money. Always be grateful for Divinity honoring your request.

Choose your best time—morning, afternoon or evening. Continue the ritual until the candle burns completely down. You are setting up the platform on the astral plane of reality for your belief through ritual. Warning: NEVER leave a candle unattended, and keep fire away from flammable items, curtains, alcohol, and more importantly, young curious children.

I taught a class in Long Beach on the history of metaphysics. One of the most interesting parts of the class was the example Aristotle used, in his book on Metaphysics, of "picking up the color red" such as depicted in your visual picture of a delicious, moist, red apple. Did you "see" the apple? Of course, you've seen it many times. My assignment for you is to "see" a stack of one hundred dollar bills, banded in groups of equal sums totaling ten thousand dollars each. You have one hundred such stacks before you, or $1 million. "See" this money in your bedroom, stacked on your bed. In your mind, stand before your bed, and as you look in amazement at your money, you may multiply it so that it goes to the roof if necessary. In this economy, a mere $1 million may not be enough! Play on your bed with the money. Use your emotions to evoke an awareness and impact from your consciousness. Tell yourself as you experience this happy feeling, "I am wealth. I am health. I am success." Whatever you place behind "I AM" becomes your truth!

There are guides, angels and earth-bound ancestors on the invisible level, guarding over your life while you are in your body. However, you are not doing this just for the wealth—you do it because you are able to help others while acknowledging a power higher than yourself. This is what is meant by saying that you "put on the Consciousness of Christ," because you become conscious of it. It is important to spend time daily in meditation regarding wealth and abundance.

Yesterday died and is gone forever; tomorrow is a future imagined; today is all there is, and all you have. Your "today" creates your tomorrow for all eternity.

Reginald G. Johnson, Ph.D

6.

Have You Walked On Water Yet?

Your psychic or mystical experience is an individual
one. There is a dynamic power inside of you, which
can transcend time, space and physical limitations.
You are powerful. Have you walked on water yet?

In the New Testament of the Scriptures, there is a story of St. Peter, a disciple of Jesus, whose desire it was to be like Him in every way—to strive for the highest level of mystical spirituality. Remember, Jesus of Nazareth and his followers were all Jewish men, and anything in the Jewish community which was "against" traditional religious beliefs was to be abolished. Imagine the look on the faces of His followers when, during a violent sea storm, they could actually see Jesus defying all the laws of physical science and gravity as He walked on water toward their fishing vessel. St. Peter thought he was seeing a *ghost*, as reported in the New Testament. This tells me they knew about ghosts and/or spirits; but it was neither elaborated on nor removed from the Scriptures. Jesus reassured them that it was He and not a "ghost." When Peter saw this feat, he attempted to duplicate it. His first attempt was successful until he "realized" his physical awareness and began to sink. He was saved and brought to safety by Christ. This is one of the most cherished Bible stories in my opinion, because it speaks of faith. This is a very sacred drama.

Some people are walking on water and others are "stuck" in the boat, while still others are sinking. Many are afraid they are going to sink in life's problems and concerns. Yes, it does take faith, according to Scripture, to please God. Something I read once said that when Jesus turned water into wine, "water" recognized who Jesus was; all the elemental properties of water aligned themselves with His faithful command, and the water "blushed" and turned into the best tasting wine ever! I thought this was beautifully poetic.

Every person on this planet must pass through some storm, challenge or incident in his or her life. The doctor may tell you about some disease in your body; you may have just heard about a parent's loss of life without your having said goodbye; you may have just lost your job (I did that—a lot! I discovered J.O.B. means "Just Over Broke"); there are lots of stormy waters in life that we have to view differently. When your personal sky gets dark and the winds begin to blow against you as you find yourself in murky water—don't be afraid! Fear not!

This is the time to walk on water. In other words, dare to confront the situation. Why? Because inside of you is the Solution, or God Consciousness. Wherever you are—God is! The Scriptures indicate this in the Old Testament. I reference the Bible because it is an amazing Book. Joshua 1:9 says it clearly: *"Be strong and of a good courage; be not afraid, neither be thou dismayed for the Lord thy God is with thee withersoever thou goest."*

You have to "recognize" the Power in you. Everthing you think about is really a prayer because "thinking is the highest form of prayer." You have to guard your thoughts judiciously and understand that you can calm the seas of trouble by learning to plant mental seed thoughts of love, protection, faith, hope, wealth, and more. Your mystical garden will produce in your life all the beautiful flowers, or visible outcome, of those thoughts. When these fishermen saw Christ standing on water, it dawned on me that He did not get into the boat with them when he was talking to them about their fears. He stood in "the midst of the storm" as a symbol of the Divine Order of consciousness, in spite of the raging winds and seas. This story not only illustrates the fear-based incidents that happen in life, or the fact that the "miracle" of walking on water defied gravitational law; I believe it helps you to overcome the focus on your surroundings and to refocus your attention on God within us as the Power. God dreamed us, and we are the offspring of Divine Mind waiting to reconnect to that Eternal Validity. We can find hope and joy amid suffering and darkness. We always live under the emblem of God.

You are spirit—linked to the Divine. When you know this, you too can "walk on water" and feel quite content in your current position or your walk. However, we all need proof! Peter said, "If it's really you, Lord, command me to come to you on the water." Jesus said, "Come." Peter believed his feet should not have been able to stand on water. He started to `believe` his outer experiences—wind, rain, stormy seas, life-threatening waves—and what happened? He lost "contact" with the "Inner" person. You are an individualized unit of consciousness. Christ came to show us this very fact. Hold onto your seatbelt because, once more, your religion is not the thing that makes you—it's your relationship to the Infinite Mind of God! Remember this always.

Stay focused and be prepared for anything. When you feel that life is making you "sink" on the waters of debt, problems, fear, unfaithfulness, divorce—this is the time to realize that you will not be distracted by outside forces and doubt (prayer in reverse); you will always remain firm and have the ability to walk on water. Let the winds come, and the trouble—you are not alone. Think of yourself as having the ability to walk on water. You belong to the Divine family of God, who never wants to see you sink but to soar to great heights. You deserve love, fulfillment, great health and wealth. Get out of the boat of fear—step out in faith and walk on water!

As a child, all I thought about was church. I loved the people, the worship, the ceremony, the stories from the Bible and the personal stories from the ministers and presenters, or guest speakers—I even loved the "smell" of church. I know—I was a weird kid. I had a lot of mystical experiences. I knew there was—and is—God. One day, as a teen, I was praying while walking from church on Third Street in northwest Washington, D.C. I know the church is still there—I spoke with my cousin, who is now 91 years of age and has finished her third book. As I looked up, I felt a strange energy all over my body, which can be described as heat surrounded by tiny pearls of ice crystals.

There was a huge cross in the sun. Why I was "allowed" to see this?I have no idea. It was a mind-blowing experience. It came directly from the sun, with the sun itself being the brightest part in the center and four solid, distinct emanations forming the sign of the cross. The sensations I remember were heat, cool, tingling and a magnetic pull. My spirit interpreted this as earth, air, fire and water. The cross pre-dates Christianity and Jesus. But I knew I had a lot of water to cross (pardon the pun) and miles to go in my life. The Christ energy is so human and divine simultaneously; there is no bias or judgment in His personality, only love. To walk on the waters of life's unpredictable seas, and stay afloat, we must adopt those principles which He displayed and all others before and after

Him who also displayed them as well. By this I mean the continuous "Divine" brotherhood of men (and women) in the past such as Buddah, Krishna, Mithras, Orpheus, Osiris, Dionysus and Adonis. There are striking similarities between the stories of Jesus and those of the last five entities mentioned, in terms of virgin births, death and resurrection. Christianity has Pagan DNA indeed. Before causing a riot, go back and read, research and pay attention to Christian history. Also, I would include mention of those modern-day mystics who paid a visit to the planet—Ghandi, Mother Theresa and even Martin Luther King, Jr.

Jesus refused to be worshipped because it was "…the Father in Me that doeth the work." We are so challenged by doubt, circumstances and daily living—especially fear—and it blinds us to who we are in God. Let us see the light and remove the blinders. You will receive a spiritual transformation, which brings great peace, and you too, can then ask, "Have you walked on water yet?"

The Holy Spirit cannot enter a mind, body or soul divided against itself. Be forgiving, non-critical, loving, healing and thoughtful of others and the Holy Spirit will come. Guaranteed.

Reginald G. Johnson, Ph.D

7.

Miracle Healing

Faith healers, shamans, American Indians, Voodoo priests and medicine men, Christian Scientists—all report miracle healing in their various religions. Healing occurs when we learn to forgive others and love others and ourselves unconditionally!

Faith healers, shamans, American Indians, voodoo priests, metaphysical men, Christian Scientists—all report miracle healings in their religions. Healing occurs when we learn to forgive others and love ourselves as well as others unconditionally. How true! I attended the healing services of a woman who used to be on television. She was a "faith healer," as some would title her. She is now on the other side, still helping and healing others for God's service. During her time on earth, I was compelled to see her because I was told that my mother was dying due to the advanced stages of cancer throughout her body. This lady's services were conducted in Pittsburgh, Pennsylvania and started in Los Angeles.

I remember informing my mom that she would be okay and not to worry; although she had already lost a great deal of weight. She had started to get dark circles under her eyes, and a pale "shallow" look as though she had been attacked by vampires; she lost her energy and was only a wispy shadow of the woman she had always been. Yet, "something" inside of me *knew* that if I went to this healing service on her behalf, a demonstration of my faith would be acknowledged and she would be healed. My dear friend, who has also crossed over to the other side of this life, Dr. Bowden, always gently reminded me, "No matter what happens to you, it is not as important as how you respond to it." I became still, and prayed, and the instinctual feeling to go to this healing service became stronger. My mom and I both agreed in prayer for her healing.

The following morning, at some ungodly hour—the birds weren't chirping yet—I left Washington, D.C. with my cousin, Manuel, to meet with a group of fellow bus passengers destined to attend the healing service. We were departing from the First Assembly Church in Virginia on our way to Pittsburgh expecting miracles. The air seemed peculiarly still as we traversed the eastern seaboard many hours into daylight. There were people anxiously waiting outside the church for the doors to open. They came from all over the United States and Canada. The church held about 7,500 members and I remember three tiers of balconies. When the ushers came outside from the church, people pushed and shoved; confusion was rampant. One of the ushers said, "Don't push others, remember the Kingdom of God is orderly." At 8:30 a.m., those who were ambulatory were directed to one side of the auditorium, while others who were not able to walk and were assisted with canes, crutches and wheelchairs were directed to the opposite side. The auditorium filled to capacity in a New York nanosecond. I was stunned—it was as though these people rehearsed all of this the week before. My cousin and I stood there speechless! There was nowhere to sit. We stood in the back of the auditorium asking for God's help. I did not travel all the way from D.C. to come away without the experience of a healing for mom. I looked up at the sea of people in this place, including those from the State of Pennsylvania from what was called "Dutch Country" in those days. I believe they are Amish. I felt an overwhelming compassion for all the people who needed healing physically, emotionally and spiritually. At that point I thought, "I wish I was on the stage with the others before the *healing lady* came out. God, what is my lesson in this?" At that moment, Manuel was tapping me on my shoulder and was telling me we were being motioned to come down on the stage by the Amish lady in the white bonnet. From the distance in the back of the auditorium, she was indicating with her index finger for me and my cousin to come down the aisle and up on stage. I pointed to myself as if to ask, "You mean me?" She nodded affirmatively. "Wow," I thought, "God answers those prayers quickly." It was like a trip to Oz. Anything seemed possible.

There were two folding chairs on stage behind the podium! We went on stage and sat there.

Once on stage, the healer entered and the entire room was quiet. The silence was deafening. You could hear a pin drop. She had on a long, white dress like a robe. As she leaned forward with her thin body, red hair and firm voice, she appeared as a goddess and said, "The Holy Spirit is in this place." Every atom of this woman's being radiated with the essence of God, which you could feel in her presence. The air was charged with the perfectly familiar, yet unexplained energy of the Divine. I knew it. After prayer, song, and adoration to God, I remember her looking up toward the balcony and saying that someone was healed of asthma after fourteen years. Some woman from the balcony was shouting praises of her healing. My cousin was more skeptical by nature. He thought it was "staged." I knew it was real. At this time, I was thinking, "How does she know these things?" She must have "felt" my thought energy as she turned in my direction, looked right through my soul with those crystal blue-green eyes and verbalized, "Young one, don't ask how I know these things. My spirit bears witness with God's Spirit."

Somebody, hurry up and purchase me for two cents—that is how I felt. I was ready to have a religious meltdown into the floor on stage. It was the most shocking, elevating and most angelic confirming experience of my life! It blew my mind. Then

74

she touched people on that first row on stage and people passed out. I remember a "floating" sensation and saw colors, and experienced a fragrance which I know does not exist on earth. I reached back to touch her and she said, "No. If you touch me, I'll go under the Power." Others touched her. Why not me?

She then said, your mother is in the hospital in Washington, D.C. People believe she is dying from cancer. I want you to accept her healing in the name of Jesus. She does not have cancer. I knew then my mom was being healed. After all the services were conducted, and people were ready to leave, there were still those who were "slain by the Spirit" and in that altered, cosmic state of consciousness which cannot be described in the human language. Finally, all attendees were headed back to their respective groups—some healed and some not healed. Again, my mental question was "Why weren't these people healed or those people healed, or that poor, innocent child?" Again, the `healing lady` "picked up" my thought wave and answered, "I don't know why God chooses to heal some and not others. It is all in His plan and time." I was freaked out enough for that one day and headed back to my own group from Virginia. There was a little boy who wanted to sit next to me on the way back home. He looked like an angel— blonde hair, large green eyes, and a cherub face.

There was obviously something wrong with his right foot because of the brace on it. Also, there was a woman on that bus who was also not healed. She was quite embarrassed because of a severe case of varicose veins. The little boy and I were looking out of the window of the bus. I noticed the combination of partly cloudy and partly clear weather.

Suddenly, a cloud covered the sun partially and several streaks of light peered through. One light in the middle of these three sunrays "moved" over toward the bus. The lady sitting near the front of the bus started screaming, shouting, crying, and moving hysterically from her seat. The driver stopped the bus trying to figure out what was happening. As she lifted her pant legs, we witnessed that her varicose veins were completely gone and her legs looked smooth.

The little boy sitting next to me was telling me to look at his foot, less dramatically than the woman was, and before my eyes (and others on this bus), his foot was making involuntary movements and there was a "crunching" sound as his leg and his foot straightened. My eyes scanned the bus observing the onlookers—some in shock and disbelief, others with tears of joy streaming down their cheeks in adoration of God's handiwork. While we paused from all the excitement, somewhere between Hershey, Pennsylvania and "Dutch" Country, I decided to use the opportunity to phone my mother from the phone booth (cell phones were not in fashion yet). Once I was able to contact her, I asked how she felt. She indicated she felt a little better, but nothing remarkable. I knew it would be eventful by the time I arrived. Once in Washington, I called her again and she was actually walking around, visiting the Pediatrics Department of the D.C. General Hospital. While my older sister, Josephine (now crossed over) thought my mother was dying, I thought she was about to live.

Later mom got better; her health improved dramatically, and the doctor, a pathologist, indicated that her healing could not be explained except by Divine intervention. I love it! That Sunday, she was an outpatient. She lived many, many years afterwards. I thanked God for her healing. My belief is that each person comes here through the mother vehicle with many angels that watch, guide, deliver, heal, uplift, and inspire—they have a lot of duties, responsibilities and influence over our daily lives. It is our responsibility to harness that energy and perfect it in ourselves. I believe that the clearer your communication with your higher perceptual nature, or angels (guides), the more dramatic your positive experience in life is.

The Shaman, Voodoo Priest, Faith Healer, Native American Medicine Man—all have one thing in common. They have learned that the higher mind is "energized" toward healing through the fuel of belief and faith. There is that sacred part of each person's being where the word "incurable" does not and cannot exist. That tremendous subconscious mind has no limits. God placed it there invisibly prior to your incarnation on earth so that you could call on it at will to cure any illness! The world will place many false beliefs from daily living in your consciousness. The powerfully negative images and words from the TV, radio and print news, if not personally filtered and reinforced with positive images coupled with self-talk, may prevent healing on many levels. Repetition creates impact. When you are bombarded with death, kidnapping, terrorism, abduction of children, fatal accidents, war, and so on, and those seed images are planted in your mind prior to sleep, imagine what grows inside of your being. "Images" are produced by thinking—your highest form of prayer. When you sleep, you don't dream in words, but in symbols or images projected from what you experienced during your daily waking hours. We must deliberately train our thoughts daily through powerful thinking for positive healing results. Make a habit of going to sleep each night with healthy thoughts for optimum health in body and mind. The mind created the body that houses the spirit.

8.

I Know What You're Thinking

Telepathy between others is a fact. A mother knows instinctively when her children are in danger, and we all "tap in" to this energy. Learn to do it at will and be "in the know."

Telepathy is real and we all "tap in" to this energy. But what is it? Telepathy is communication from mind to mind or soul to soul without any visible means of physical contact. Contact, however, is very real. When you pray, you contact your Higher Self, or the part that God placed in you, giving you an answer according to your belief system. Try this prayer: "The light of God goes before me and clears my path, making my day abundant, loving, happy and prosperous; the beautiful sacred light of Love surrounds me, and I am always protected by this Supernatural Force charged with beauty." Do you realize that if you repeat this prayer daily, it is an act of communication with Infinite Intelligence? This affirms your belief in your subconscious mind, which knows all, sees all, and responds to your belief. Action and reaction are real, eternal, universal and cosmic. When we realize that we are Divine in our being, we make it an active part of our true nature; we will

79

stop seeing the "one-sided" energy of God, but will know that this Energy is as close as the next breath we take. Then, and only then, does life itself have purpose and conviction.

The Bible calls the inner God-self the "I AM." The Energy of God is very personal. It cannot be created or destroyed—it just is! When we lose our sense of fear, and yield to the inner God-urge to form us to our full potential, it is the most liberating sensation on the planet. This God consciousness is living "as you" in this incarnation. Everything you think will cause the mind of God consciousness in you to respond accordingly.

As I often tell my students, in the realm of mind-spirit, there is no "time or distance.". When my mother passed over to the next dimension of life, my sister Janet "saw" her appear at her apartment in Washington, D.C. I was very close to my mother, and she knew I would contact her in the future; however, she manifested so that my sister would have confirmation of her ongoing existence. On the other hand, my father showed up in a dream one night—I picked up telepathic messages from him on the other side. This dream was so real, I asked him what he was doing in the house, because he had "died." That was surreal. It did not frighten me, it just did not make sense. He appeared to tell me goodbye because when I traveled to see him he had already "crossed over."

Every person is Spirit first and then who they are. You are mystical, psychic, magical, and everything else in that realm.

How many times have you thought of someone, and that v person called you on the phone? You possess powers that are yet untapped or neglected. As you grow in spirit—through prayer, meditation, affirmation and study, these "powers" will increase tremendously. **All spiritual work, whether from a mystical, Wiccan, Christian, pagan, Shaman or any other viewpoint should be done only in love and with the power of love.** Anything else crosses the border to the "dark side" and will come back to overshadow you in the highest negative manner.

Meditation can also assist you in your spiritual development. However, it requires focus and discipline. I meditate every morning before my workday begins and each evening as the last thing on my mind before retiring. God's supernatural energy is with you and in you now.

Exercise *(remember: you may tape record your session)*: Relax your body from head to toe. Relax your mind while burning incense or a candle; gently focus on your thoughts. "See,"in your mind's eye, a bright, neon-white light around your body. Pay attention to body sensations—changes in temperature or feelings. Release your attachment to the physical world. That includes boyfriend, girlfriend, career, job stress, etc. Feel this beautiful energy of love and warm light from the top of your head, moving gently downward with streams of love on your face, neck, shoulders, arms, forearms, ack—moving in sheets of love to the remainder ...ouy to the feet, without a care in the world.

Take a deep breath in through your nose, holding it to the mental count of 5—4—3—2—1; repeat this three times, pausing, allowing your body and mind to relax. Now imagine your energy, thoughts, and focus drifting and spiraling down into the earth as you remain aware of your breathing—deeply and slowly. Let your consciousness come to rest inside the earth where you find a beautiful stone. You feel attached to this stone. It pulsates with its own energy and light. Feel it all over your body including your feet. Feel the energy radiating all over your body while your consciousness feels the warmth and love of mother Earth. You feel grounded and protected by the vibrations of this stone emanating the energy of Mother Earth which feeds the world and everyone on this plane. Sense the warm light tingling from your feet to the scalp. Sense a beautiful, brilliant red pulsating cord of energy from your reproductive organs connecting you with the Earth. Feel the energy of the stone pulsate more rapidly as you know you are connected by love to the earth. Put your stone back in its place where you can always return when you feel the need for grounding. Be aware of your breathing and the feeling of relaxation.

Stay connected to the energy of the grounding cord and imagine floating upwards form the earth back to your own personal energy field. Know that you are protected by Mother Earth's grounding ability to sustain and keep you healthy. On the count of 5—4—3—2—1 you feel refreshed, grounded and ready to do any spiritual or stress-related activity.

Your subconscious mind believes this exercise because it appears very real. The more you do this, the more grounded and "psychic" you become. With repeated practice on a daily basis, of no more than 10 to 15 minutes a day, it will increase your vibration and allow you to enter the fourth dimension of your higher self, which responds according to your belief and recognition of the Presence of God. When you do this, the subconscious mind becomes the guiding principle to allow you to see events from the past, present or future—making you aware and awake.

Always say a prayer for Divine love and protection as you enter your meditative or psychic state of awareness. Awaken each morning with "an attitude of gratitude to increase your latitude." This is the sacred circle of God's power and love which surrounds you. Action and reaction are universal and have cosmic significance. You will not "create" Energy, neither will you destroy It. You will know that Energy is—and you will develop the power to impress upon this energy to cause a reaction. You are merely impressing the energy of God with your mind. Be more receptive—not aggressive, on this new level of reality.

We are infinite beings having a human experience. Physical fitness starts with spiritual fitness, and thereafter, mental fitness, which trickles down to the body reflecting perfect health. Again, do not exclude medical science or doctors who learn all their lives. Hopefully, your doctor is spiritually inclined and will look at the root mental cause of any physical or psychic illness, seeing the body-spirit dichotomy, recognizing it for what it is in your goal toward wellness and away from negative spiritual invasions.

When you become aware of the Presence of the Spirit of God in your body, knowing you are expressing your individuation in the form of God clothed in your body, something magical happens; you become amazingly fit from the spiritual perspective. People will notice it and witness the presence of God in you! What you affirm with belief, fueled by faith, will manifest itself in your life.

You are immortal spirit clothed in a mortal body. You move your mind from sickness to health; from poverty to wealth; from sorrow to joy and from death to life. You are the mirrored image of God in a unitized particle of consciousness, able to mend time, photons, and electrons—doing things on another level of intelligence that is Infinite and without limitation. Your mind now becomes focused and you, too, can experience the achievement of confidence and spiritual fulfillment; with that you can say, "I know what you're thinking."

In my psychic development and meditation class, I always ask students to sit comfortably erect without arms and legs crossed, to allow the perfect flow of energy throughout the body. Always protect yourself with the earlier exercise we did with the white light. Some will do this automatically. This is called claircognizance, or an "inner knowing."

Sometimes in meditation, focus is somewhat difficult because your "left" brain does not want to accept or believe in something it cannot perceive on the physical plane. You must train it in a loving manner, recognizing any jumbled thoughts of consciousness that float through in your energy field; see it for what it is and move on lovingly. *Meditation increases your psychic awareness.* Try to meditate at the `same time` each day so that your mind and the atmospheric condition of meditation are more powerful. You are expanding ethereal, sacred energy and this becomes your power base.

In time of war, pray for peace, not revenge. The Prince of Peace, the Christ Consciousness, will lead you and the nation toward that goal.

Reginald G. Johnson, Ph.D

9.

Becoming Enlightened

Enlightenment is a state of spiritual awareness and knowledge, which is different for each person. You are a spirit first—then you are who you are. You are a living soul who is born with inner wisdom from God. Learn to use it with the most powerful force in the galaxy—love.

There may be a new book inside of you, or a Broadway play, musical compositions, movie, or invention—all will be channeled from God directly to you! On the road to enlightenment, using consciousness in an effort to bring us back to the perceptual reality of our relationship with Father/Mother God, we begin to fully realize who we are.

Enlightenment, which is as varied as each individual's fingerprint, is an experience of regaining our perfection in God or Christ consciousness, and words alone cannot express the joyfulness and peace in that discovery. God energy is perfect energy, and because we are God's offspring, so are we perfect. Standard religious beliefs try to convince us that this perfection is achieved somewhere in the "by and by." However, there is a

Bible passage, which says, "Be `perfect`, therefore, as your heavenly Father is `perfect`." Matthew 5:48.

There is only one God in reality. Remember, we are created in the `image` and `likeness` of God (Genesis 1:26-27). Some academic folk, theologians, and TV evangelists would lead you to believe that the Bible meant something totally different than what the *New Age people* try to tell us, and they will "explain" in the light of their own conclusions as well.

We are a part of the Mind that created time and space. This may be a difficult concept for some to grasp. However, the important thing to grasp in our four-dimensional space-time continuum is that you are part of the Divine Principle and always will be. What makes you who you are is your relationship with God. You have worth and unique value in the entire Universe. Your REAL being is Spirit—God can only produce God or Itself. Every seed produces its own kind—including humans. We are a combination of matter and spirit. You are an expression of God, not God Himself 100%. That is why it is difficult for any psychic to be 100% accurate all the time!

Enlightenment is becoming our God-selves manifested on earth. It is the process of becoming God thinking, God producing, God loving and God giving. Everything and everybody returns to God who gave life to all. We were ideas in the Mind of God and came to earth.

You are a living soul born with inner wisdom from God. Learn to use it with the most powerful force in the galaxy—Love.

There are many avenues leading to the road of enlightenment. Meditation and prayer are two of the most powerful. But as you have noticed, you must ground and center yourself in meditation. This should be a self-enforced discipline on a daily basis. In meditation, your number-one purpose is for enlightenment and attaining wisdom, truth and perfection.

Every particle of your being will vibrate in unison and harmony with the invisible world on the astral plane. Always eliminate any negative energy first—burn incense, use protection oils, light candles, and use other divinatory means of protection. You may call on your particular guides and angels to guide you.

I notice in my classes, or other sacred circles, that there is a major respect for the Holy Spirit regardless of religious background. We glorify the unity of God and realize our connection with the energy of God. When we realize our "God" energy, you can actually feel the Holy Spirit in the room.

Faith is an important element in attaining enlightenment. "Be it done unto you according to your faith," was something quoted often by Christ. Faith is an attitude and a way of thinking. When you "know" something and emotionalize and feel it to be true, it will be impressed on the subconscious level of mind which affects the astral level. It impregnates the deeper mind with the strategy of your intent—making it objectified, physical reality on the earth plane. It has been impressed on the Universal screen. You come from a Creator; therefore, you have the ability to create.

If I were a medical doctor, I would have faith in medicine and medical principles that have been proven. If an attorney, I would have faith in the justice system and jury. As a minister and teacher, I have to have faith in God. My alignment must be perfect. I ask and pray that you, too, have faith in the God of your understanding and belief. Spiritual conviction is a prerequisite, which begins in the mind. Your attitude and mental conviction about the laws of your spirit and mind will be as Christ stipulated in Mark 9:23, "If you can believe, ALL things are possible."

There is a sacred wisdom inside of you at the time of your conception through the mother vehicle to this plane called earth. As you are alive, you are animated with eternal truth within yourself. There is a reality that can never be explained away. The most intelligent scientist on the planet will never be able to figure out, explain, or comprehend the profundity, magnitude or magnificence of God who created his or her being in the first place.

"Why are your prayers always answered?" asked a friend of mine of many years. "You asked for an office which was occupied at the time, and declared it was yours, and that happened; you said you would manifest a five-bedroom house from a two-bedroom apartment and you did." My response to him was "You are rewarded for your faith and the law works when you believe. As a mystic and child of God (and Goddess—because God has simultaneous male and female energy)—the law works for everyone, just as the law of lightning works on the physical plane and will strike you whether you are "aware" of the law or not. The law of good works on the plane of the invisible.

Shakespeare said "All things be ready if the mind be so." If your mind is ready and your spirit is open to receive, all you have to do is speak the word. When your mind and heart believe in reality what you are thinking to yourself and what you say out loud, that becomes your planted, growing, sprouting, outward reality for all to see. It takes on an incredible amount of speed by the food and fuel fed to it by your power. If you are not ready for that experience, you have to nurture it with prayer and meditation. It then becomes formula, which needs to be repeated daily and freely in a loving, joyous manner.

The Bible is amazing as a teaching tool for the laws of the Universe. In Genesis, or the beginning, it says, "God **said** *Let there be light*," and there was light; "God **said** *Let* **us** *make man;*" and man was created. To apply our own spiritual success as the Spirit of God working in us, we have to

think, say and believe in our higher selves for achievement and success on the spiritual, mental and physical levels. Faith is key to achievement of any goal in life. You cannot conduct any business without faith that you will be successful based on your plans and execution of those plans. Just let go and let God!

You have learned a very powerful lesson. In order to become enlightened, you are building the qualities and characteristics necessary for your mystical abilities. My students know that they travel out of their bodies to the fourth dimension. I explain to them that when they are in a deep state of sleep, they unconsciously leave the body and travel to the fourth dimension where all the answers to life's problems exist.

While traveling back and forth between the fourth dimension and the third, where physical activity is located—your heart rate, respiration, perspiration, circulation—the blood in the body travels upside down against the physical laws of gravity, miraculously working in Divine order while you are having an out-of-body experience (OBE). You may have questions about the most perplexing life problems, and the answers will be given to you in symbols and dreams.

You should always keep your dream journal next to your bed, because the pattern formed will reveal valuable information to you.

You can tune in to your enlightenment.

forms a vibration at the highest level of influei

dimension. Which means, in simple terms, thou◡   ⌐al

and thoughts are things. They impress the vibration on the submind or unconsciousness. What you do in your actions is the three-dimensional form of prayer in action. If you think good or positive thoughts—your actions will be positive.

There is a statement in the Book of Proverbs, twenty-third chapter, seventh verse: "*For as a man thinketh in his heart, so is he.*" What do you think about all day? What do you say to yourself and others? Your enlightenment comes when you realize that you have no control over other people, but you have control over how you respond to other people. If you judge them, even in gossip, you judge God who made them and God who is in them. Remember, your thinking is the highest form or prayer. The Presence of God is right where you are. All the qualities and aspects of God and Goddess, or male and female energy of God, are inside of you and deeply buried in your subconscious mind.

After you have centered yourself and quietly selected your sacred space where you will not be disturbed, burning a white candle or uplifting, fragrant incense, say aloud and repeat to yourself: "THERE IS PEACE AROUND ME; GOD IS WHERE I AM NOW. THE HOLY SPIRIT (OR GODDESS, or other name for God) IS IN THIS PLACE. I HAVE PEACE; I HAVE LOVE; I

VE UNDERSTANDING. I AM WEALTHY, I AM INTUITIVE, I AM IN GREAT HEALTH."

You may not believe this mantra, but say it until it is ingrained in your consciousness before falling asleep. When you awaken, notice different vibrations and a sense of newness and serenity in your room. Do this each night. Remember, when working with candles, never leave them burning unattended. Feel the presence in the room.

When you are on the road to enlightenment, your faith is placed in your Higher Self. When you become enlightened, you view the world differently. For example, you have a friend who is hit by a car and fatally wounded; or a family member has a heart attack or cancer. Some people respond, "How could God let this happen?" Or, "She was such a religious person, how could God let her die?" God is not responsible for anyone's demise or destruction. That is not an excuse for apathy. On the contrary, every person has the capacity to choose to direct his or her life by his or her own free will. Your thinking makes you happy, sad, well, or sick. This has been proven. There is an Old Testament scripture in the Book of Isaiah: Isaiah 30:15 "In quietness and in confidence shall be your strength." This is how you know who you are and your growth in God. You do not own a person. Even your own children are "on loan" to you from God to learn their own lessons of success, failure, growth, surrender, and love—love being the most powerful.

When you realize that God is always God no matter what—and you claim God as the Source and validity of who you are—you "add life to your being" as well as "years and health to your life." It is your responsibility to "tune in" to the frequency of God in you. You are not a robot, but a spirit expressing yourself in human form. You were born as a beautiful spirit—a unit of awareness or consciousness with the ability to choose. What will you choose today?

My mother used to always say, "God is no respecter of persons." This statement comes from the Bible. I know that this is true. I also heard another New Testament statement over and over; when I was challenged in my faith and reported this to my parents, they retorted, "It rains on the just and the unjust." In other words, everybody has the ability to mentally make choices, and good as well as bad things happen to "good" people. However, when you realize that God is represented as YOU—a unique unit of awareness with the "image" and "likeness" of God, then comes your enlightenment. God never changes—you can put money on that! You have to know that you can change by the power of your mind, soul and spirit. Nothing controls you or your life but you. Place your confidence and your faith in the Presence of God inside of you. Christ said the Kingdom of God is within. People (who are spirits first) can usually tell when you have made that connection. They subconsciously realize your intent, which cannot be faked.

97

When you align with God in a sincere way, it will shine through your body, and the power and laws of attraction will draw people to you. You are working your enlightened magic from the inside—out!

If you seek the approval of others, your "light" of awareness needs to be turned on.

Reginald G. Johnson, Ph.D

10.

Earth, Air, Fire and Water

All things are composed of these essential magical elements— earth, air, fire and water. Each age and leader—whether magi, saint or miracle worker—has learned this secret and controls it wisely to improve the quality of life on earth for man.

What do these symbols of earth, air, fire and water represent? They represent realms, kingdoms and boundaries in the mystical sense. In the Universe, these are the building blocks of which all things are made. The ancient, earth-based religions, such as Wicca, Celtic Magick, and Native American sacred traditions, as well as intelligent twenty-first century mystics, realize that the element of `air` represents the intellect. This corresponds to the east. The color associated with this element in many spiritual circles is yellow, representing "Divine intelligence." Notice the yellow halo around the paintings of Jesus, Mary and the patron saints. In some instances it is represented as the color blue, which I also find interesting because the Native Americans referred to this element as "Father Sky."

..... element of `earth` is related to the direction of the north. It represents the material world—foundation, ground and body.

The colors of earth are black, brown, and green. The ground itself has a brown hue, out of which sprouts green grass and plants; look at the trees for the earth's representation of growth. "Mother" earth embodies fertility, nurturing and growth.

The element of `water,` which corresponds to the direction of the west, is represented in colors of light green and silver. This energy represents the emotions, intuition and the subconscious mind. In the Christian tradition, it represents the ritual of baptism, or entry into purification and cleansing in the watery grave of Christ.

The element of `fire`, represented as the direction of south as well as the color red, reflects desire, passion, energy, determination, the human will, and ambition. Fire purges and cleanses. Anything that goes through fire must change. In the Bible, particularly the New Testament, the Holy Spirit is associated with Fire (and for those who do not remember, the ancient Hebrew text shows the Holy Spirit as female). There were at Pentecost "tongues of fire" which appeared on the heads of those present in their belief and faith; also there was a sound as of the "rushing wind," which is interesting when you compare the Holy Spirit to Comforting and Cleansing.

All religions, which are man-made, have a common thread that connects each expression handed down from the ancestors demonstrating their theories, ways of life and beliefs common to their culture. There is a `fifth element` added to the four previously mentioned, which is "spirit" binding the others.

These elements or "life energies" also correspond to the Tarot and to Astrology. For example, in the Tarot deck, wands are represented by the element of fire; the cups represent water; the swords represent the element of air; and the coins or pentacles symbolize earth. There are, of course, corresponding astrological signs of `fire` (Aries, Leo, Sagittarius); `water` (Cancer, Scorpio and Pisces); `air` (Gemini, Libra, Aquarius); and `earth` (Taurus, Virgo, Capricorn). Would it not be interesting to discover which of the twelve disciples Jesus selected who represented each of these elements? I smell research! These are all the cosmic, divine energies of God with which all religions have a connection.

You are the offspring of the one Cosmic Creator in the Universe. Some of us are more connected than others. It is a matter of perception and your ability to grow in consciousness. In one of my meditations on the elements of earth, air, fire and water, it was revealed to me how some ancient, invisible angelic energies "fell from grace" and became jealous of man at creation when the Creator did the unthinkable—combined matter, elements and spirit, making man. It was a pretty intense meditation. Whether this is the case or not is conjecture, of course. But the impact was lasting.

God is Divine on equal footing as male and female and does not "send people to hell"; that is self-imposed by your belief. Therefore, if someone approaches me and speaks of Goddess worship, I am smart enough to know that this is not new. Mother Earth as Goddess was later evolved to the Virgin Mary because of the influence of Christianity. She represents "nurturing, comfort and protection" as do all wives, sisters and mothers. Sacred masculinity and sacred femininity co-exist in consciousness. The Female Slavery 101 Course is no longer available. Men in ancient times made it difficult for women to practice their beliefs because they believed women were not on equal ground. The sacred energies of the elements are in everyone.

In ancient spiritual history (Hebrew mysticism and esoteric philosophy) there is something called the Tetragrammaton, which refers to Yod Heh Vau Heh (YHVH)—translated as Jehovah, and comprising qualities representing earth, air, fire and water. You are the fifth element—spirit or ether.

I find it interesting how Moses of the Bible is connected with the symbolism of the color red. The wand, or staff (more Biblically appropriate), represents the fire element. His cloak further symbolized fire by its red color. His life in the desert, with its red sands and blazing sun, evokes further in heat and red.

The "burning bush" which was not consumed is another such symbol, as is the "shining countenance" of Moses. The film version of the story shows the Ten Commandments being "etched and burned into the mountainside" by the finger of God, with a fiery laser splendor of cosmic proportions. Additionally, a pillar of fire appeared in the desert before Moses (another obvious symbol of fire); and he held a wand (fire/red) with which he touched and parted the "Red" Sea. All these facts of association reflect a beautiful story of connection and a passion for the voice of God.

As a Pisces (water sign), born February 28, I am naturally intuitive. This is very true in my case. Many clients from the East and West Coasts of the United States consult me for my divine connection with God, for which I am extremely grateful. The element water is also very powerful because it represents symbols, dreams, the unconscious, and the watery depths of emotion and feeling. Other associations of water are love and hope. The sacred chalice is another symbol for water signs. In the New Testament, don't you find it interesting how Jesus is associated with water? Look at the symbols:

> He changed water into wine (His first "miracle").
> He walked on water to the astonishment of his followers.
> He commanded the wind and seas to "be still."

)

ιe ground and made spitballs to cure a

ɔnnection to the symbols of water? Also,

ɉe of Pisces!! Irony?

During my monthly New Moon Rituals to increase prosperity and banish negativity, I ask, invite and invoke the Four Guardian Angels to attend my ceremony and they always do, without fail. Some people have a problem with calling Angels. But alas! Jesus himself said he could have called ten thousand angels. You shall do these things and greater works shall ye do! These angelic beings are the power points of earth, air, fire and water. To soothe the intense energy that fills the room, I invite the Holy Spirit and she shows up and shows out! Miracles always happen. There is only love in these rituals. Nothing is ever done to discount honor and holiness to God. People from all walks of life and faiths receive blessings.

The elements represent equal balance on all four sides of the Universe. They protect and empower us. When you pray, try something different. If you employ the symbol of "crossing your heart" and verbalize Father, Son, Holy Spirit, Amen—try saying and thinking the Powers of Earth, Air, Fire and Water. Call forth these angels. Acknowledge them and thank them for coming to answer your prayers. Be attentive to your surroundings and watch the difference in lights, feeling, or sensation. It is amazing how your life will be changed and empowered by God. If you are "awakened" you will know this already and it will feel familiar and comforting to you. Pay attention to the way you sleep and how "balanced" it makes you feel to do this. It will be easier to meditate, calling these elemental powers and Angels.

Always place your awareness with these high, invisible and protective God forces when you travel, feel threatened, or need help—focus and call on the Angels of earth, air, fire and water. They are guardians who have been around since the creation of the world and they are with you always. The Spirit of God (and Goddess) is bound or boxed in by religious belief. God still creates and still answers prayer. Your relationship with the Divine should be a moment-by-moment spiritual experience.

Although astrology is a very viable, intuitive art, this book is not a book on the subject and I will not get into it here, but will provide a general synopsis of the elements and their representative energies.

The *"Fire"* signs are **Aries, Leo and Sagittarius**. People born under this astrological configuration are said to display assertiveness, passion, creativeness, and major leadership skills. During that time of Pentecost in the Bible when the "tongues of fire" appeared on the believers in God, what color immediately comes to mind? If you said anything other than red, you need a counseling session with me or a serious spiritual development class.

Water is necessary for life on earth. Our physical bodies are comprised mostly of this life-giving element. The *"Water"* signs are Cancer, Scorpio and Pisces. They say we are, as a whole, very sensitive. As for myself, my wife Cynthia can testify to this fact. We are largely intuitive, with strong (sometimes larger than life) imaginations. Generally, we are very people-oriented, and most water-born people have great sales skills. Of course, this all depends on the individuation of the person. You should always decide your truth! Who has not heard of "holy" water?

Water symbolizes purification, consecration, and tranquility or cleansing. This symbol is all about transformation and spirituality. Was not the Christ all of these things? Again, is this irony? Go back and study the contrasts in personality between Moses and the "fire" qualities and Jesus with the "water" personality. They both symbolized and acted on their allegiance, commitment and ultimate ascension to Divinity.

Look again at the symbol of Pisces and the Fish. Did it say in the Scriptures that Jesus fed the multitude with a few fish? Besides the cross, the symbol of the fish is a sacred one in Christianity.

Our great Mother *"Earth"* has signs of her own to boast about. They are Taurus, Virgo (my wife, Cynthia), and Capricorn. The earth is practical and they say this is true of Taurus people. Everyone knows about Virgos being "organized"—my wife can drive me to utter distraction with it sometimes. Thank God we communicate telepathically and send "love notes" to each other on the psychic level. Capricorns believe they rule the universe. In reality, they rule their own world and can be high achievers. The earth signs balance everything with their love.

Breathe in "Air" deeply and relax. These people are awesome communicators, and when you think they are not listening to you, they can repeat every word verbatim. Of course, they are represented astrologically as Gemini, Libra and Aquarius. I won't "go there" with Libras, but it's all about the money and balancing the checkbook. I know a ton of teachers and doctors who happen to be Aquarius. They can be intense outside to protect themselves, but loving on the inside!

Overall, these astrological configurations are unique, but YOU decide your fate and how you live your life by your Free Will to change your mind and your life!

When early man identified the importance of these "elements" and the laws of the universe, each culture on earth organized and formed their own systems, beliefs and religions based on how the elements operated and affected them. Therefore, it is your modern-day responsibility, as it was for our forebears and the earliest earth dwellers, to awaken those latent powers; to perceive beyond physical reality in developing your relationship with and recognizing the truth of earth, air, fire and water in your own being. Read books on Earth-based religions, Native American traditions, meditation, comparative religion, Christianity and mythology. You will find very similar, yet ancient truths about the elements and God (or Goddess), as a continuous running thread of hidden reality in each. Ultimately, you represent God on earth as yourself right now; you are composed of the cosmic elements and the earthly ones and you are awesome!

Every religion on this planet has always had supernatural "heroes" with outstanding mystical and psychic powers to keep spiritual advancement on this planet. If you can, study their astrological signs and the represented "element" to determine the inner cosmic truth of these individuals. Above all else, they did not judge others for their differences, but they knew they were here as cosmic and Divine messengers to provide the greater good for all involved. These intelligent men and women realized that they could not create God or destroy God—but could subconsciously impress this Energy called God with faith! Now the magic (and the truth) begins! You are endowed with Infinite Intelligence. This Unlimited Power without time or space is inside of you. What will you do with this power today—the fifth element—Spirit?

We are made in the image and likeness of God. Therefore, that part of you which is Divine must know the Father. Find, and use that Divine kinship.

Reginald G. Johnson, Ph.D

11.

The Power of Ritual

Ritual is a form of prayer that has "come to life" by practice. Repetition of ritual creates impact in the visible and invisible worlds. Learn the secrets of powerful rituals to transform your life.

As humans, we are the species that uses symbols. Other animals use familiar signs, landmarks and gestures given by us, or act purely on instinct. Like humans, they too have rituals of gathering food, procreation and even death rituals.

Early in the morning, take ten deep breaths in appreciation for awakening on a brand new day, under a brand new sky with opportunities to start again with a different attitude—one of gratitude. Every action that you perform in ritual has a deep meaning and impact. Although you may not perceive it on the physical level, it does have astral power. There are many unseen forces, whether earthbound or angelic, participating with you upon invitation and invocation. They are there, always watching and participating when the intention is right. I always call on the forces or angels of Earth, Air, Fire and Water. In addition, those in attendance at the New Moon Rituals know that something else happens when the Holy Spirit is called and strongly, yet lovingly participates in these events. There have been reports of healings, financial increase, returned items, loved ones found safely and a host of other "miraculous" events.

Take a look at some religious beliefs and the symbols and rituals associated with each. What do you visualize and feel when you see the following words:

- Buddha
- Wicca (Witchcraft)
- Krishna
- Vishnu
- Jesus
- Priest
- Gospel
- Pope?

There are, of course, significantly more examples of symbols which can be used, because there are so many beliefs and religions. Religion is learned and becomes incredible when understood, believed and practiced. When not understood, it can become misplaced and misleading to the individual. The rituals and symbols are there to assist in accepting varying assumptions or supporting and creating inner harmony, peace and ultimate alignment with God.

Too much emphasis should not be placed on symbols because your relationship with God (or your perception of

Divinity) should not be overshadowed by the symbols intended to invoke the presence of God to you and in you.

The subconscious mind understands and accepts symbols and ritual as very real and will mirror that reality on the physical level in your experience. The purpose of ritual is to strike a balance in spiritual attainment—whether psychic development or achievement of Christ Consciousness. Only you can achieve and master perfection of your spiritual goals. Prayer, chanting, meditation and ritual are ultimately performed to achieve unity with the Divine.

For true spiritual growth, practice is the key and so is persistence. If you are Christian this week and Wiccan next week, then "Houston, we have a problem." Why? Because rituals and symbols fueled with action and belief must be consistent for them to be actualized.

If you read the sacred text of the Bible, you find that Jesus declared often, "Be it done unto you according to your faith." What a tremendous example of Divine conduct, discipline and unconditional love Jesus was, through his use of rituals, symbols and prayer. When ritual and symbols became too theological and extreme, he rejected the priests of the day and placed importance instead on *right action*—the ultimate ritual.

Unfortunately, many well-meaning "religious" folk in traditional faiths have become spiritually shipwrecked by one-sided "my way only" belief systems.

Prayer is a ritual and "link" to the Divine. Buddah, too, rejected fussy, intensely cerebral ritual of the Hindus during his time, replacing them with his EIGHT-FOLD PATH TO ENLIGHTENMENT:

1. Right View
2. Right Aim
3. Right Speech
4. Right Action
5. Right Livelihood
6. Right Effort
7. Right Thought
8. Right Contemplation

Divine action carries a greater impact than words. Many people have invited me to read the Bhagavad-Gita, which beautifully teaches the profound selflessness of attaining union with God. However, most religions have beautiful sayings and actions for unifying with God. Find the religion and ritual you feel the greatest comfort with. Don't judge yourself. God knows who you are and will assist you in your search.

No religion works for personal growth unless right action is intended. You cannot love God and hate your neighbor. Divided kingdoms do not last.

In my studies of Wicca, or "Craft" of the wise, I found that it is an amazing belief system, which out of reverential respect for nature's beauty, consistency, and color—in the sunshine, moon, storms, stars and rivers—evolved into the varying aspects of God (gods), or Divine aspects of God. There could not have been God without Goddess, or the Great Mother. Many of the great religions on earth have been greatly influenced by Witchcraft, including Christianity. For example, there is a statement in the Bible which stipulates "As Above, So Below." That is an ancient Wiccan saying. Remember, I saw a bumper sticker and repeated it to several Wiccan clients which read, "Christianity has Pagan DNA." Wicca is a peaceful religion that respects life and nature.

Ritual is necessary to awaken deeper levels of your own consciousness. You use everything—sense, sights, chants, fragrances or any number of *cues* that you evoke to deepen your own awareness and contact your levels of knowing to make change occur in yourself and your world. Rituals are not mere mindless exercises to effect change. You must be consciously aware and disciplined for change to occur. There is a thin veil or membrane between physical life as we know it and spiritual reality. In Wicca, the festival of Samhaim (which is pronounced SOW-WEN), occurs at Halloween, or October 31st, and it is believed that at this Feast of the Dead, souls are closest to the earth by way of this thin membrane. It is

117

celebrated (symbolically) by the death of the Sun God into the land of youth where he awaits union and rebirth of the Mother Goddess. Regardless of your belief, we have the opportunity to remember our loved ones and friends "on the other side," as we honor them. If I shared this information with some of my "not so open" and straight-laced religious friends, I would be banished from earth as a heretic.

It should be our mutual (human) goal that despite our differences and affiliations, we should provide combined, positive sources of spiritual energy and inspiration to renew our lives on the planet.

Meditation means different things to people worldwide. I offer guided meditation in my classes and more advanced learning in the Mystery School. Students are guided on an inner, exploratory visual exercise. Some of the students experience Divinity when they receive messages in an open state of consciousness to God. We listen to God and trust in that Higher Self. Some tell me that in their inner landscape, they have the assistance of Angels, Guides and Ascended Masters. Some Christian views may oppose the calling of Angels. But why would Jesus indicate He could have "called ten thousand Angels" if we could not "do these things and greater things?" I have been a mystic, or psychic, for many years and have known about this gift at a young age. I also knew about the reality of spirits on the other side. In my experience with advanced souls and Angels, the have always been those of comfort, reassurance, ...u most importantly, love—rather than damnation, burning in hell, or destruction and serving God by *force*. The original Christian teachings came from God through the person of Christ and did not deal with fear, but inner wisdom.

In understanding and performing ritual, you become the filter for the other side of life. If you have fear, guilt, shame, doubt or any negative feelings or emotions (*energy in motion*)—eliminate these prior to ritual. Otherwise, they become difficult for the spirit of God to filter through to assist in your needs. This, of course, does not discount the ability of God or of "miracles." It does require you to go for five minutes a day, increasing to fifteen minutes a day, in silent reflection, prayer and meditation with God.

When meditation is successful, three components are in force:

(1)   your body (Become perfectly still, inhaling deeply to release tension.)

(2)   your mind (Become aware of brilliant white light surrounding your body; this light of God is Universal and you may call on it as the Holy Spirit or Goddess energy. If you cannot visualize it, "sense" it surrounding you as you open your heart and feel love for everything that has life.)

(3)   your spirit (Choose to tune into the higher realms of light, love and wisdom as the love of God being broadcast directly to your spirit. This opens you to receive assistance in your spiritual growth and expansion of consciousness.)

Meditation and prayer is how humans talk to God—intuition is God responding.

Consider the rituals we take for granted—baptism (water purification to protect from sin), marriage (the union and sacred contract between man and wife before God), lovemaking (the intoxicating shifting of awareness into pleasure between two lovers, traditionally to bring forth more life), watching television, going to work, driving to the grocery store, or going out to dinner. These are all rituals.

From the esoteric perspective, ritual is designed to successfully impact spiritual growth, understanding and commitment to God while in your body on the planet. Ritual is to remind you of your integral part in the mysterious continuum of life which is much larger than this reality. Your organic self-observation of who you are permits you to participate in ritual only on that level. However, you will bridge and accelerate reality on the astral plane, with practice, to eliminate the barrier or restrictive falseness between yourself and what we call God.

In the Christian religion, with its wisdom and knowledge, observe the pursuit of ritual in the act of salvation, regardless of how it is meant to be understood. First there is the "altar call" for all sinners to come and receive forgiveness of their sins, through Christ; then there is either an announcement or prayer to invoke Christ into the person's life; then the former sinner must confess he is a sinner and must confess Jesus as Lord (or God, Savior) and, depending on the particular belief, later get "baptized" and receive "the Holy Ghost."

I have come to terms with my own salvation, managing entry into the higher realms and mastery over substance on this planet with the use of Alchemy—transforming the rugged spirit into a sparkling, radiant diamond! Speaking of transformation, the amazing beauty rituals women go through to look good for men and to maintain our interest is nothing short of magical. They go to bed appearing one way and in the morning, can transform at will into visions of magnificence.

God loves you whether the ritual is a simple prayer or an advanced exercise in magick or Wicca. It is your intent. As a human, it is difficult to achieve mastery in every part of your life. But please master the daily ritual of a thankful heart, a loving smile, a greeting to a neighbor and a song to the Universe.

My clients who seek financial and other forms of prosperity ask me about the candle ritual. In this ritual, I etch the symbol of the dollar sign ($) into the wax of a green candle. I then ask the client how much money they are seeking. I then inscribe that amount into the wax. I also inform her or him that they must believe that they deserve this amount. Patchouli oil (usually two drops) "seals" the money into the ritual candle. I take two more drops of the money-attracting oil and stroke the candle on the opposite side in a downward motion. I request that the client burn the candle at the same time of day or night, to allow the "left brain" to accept ritual without mental distraction. Next, I place the candle in the client's "active" hand, or hand they write with, and call on the powers of the Angels of Earth, Air, Fire and Water. As soon as I call on the Holy Spirit, an obvious warmth travels through my hands into my client's hands and the candle. After a period of thirty days, the first stage of wealth benefits begin to manifest.

Wealth is not the only request of my clients, however. Some need special prayer; others ask me to perform a house-warding ritual to release negative energy and spirits from their homes; still others need to balance the chakras, or the life energy centers that flow in and out of our aura or "life force" of the body. The ritual is much more effective when the client is relaxed and receptive to this ritual, or any ritual.

Ritual brings us into alignment with the power of God—the ultimate awareness. Once alignment is attained, there is a breakthrough of understanding on all levels and you will evoke material transformation in your character. We all have that ability and are linked on the Pathway of Energy to who God is, whether through salvation, mediumship, meditation or telepathy—it is up to you to find it, and you will.

Reginald G. Johnson, Ph.D

It rains on the "just" and the "unjust" as well as the good, bad and ugly. The sun doesn't shine only on your garden. It does so on friendly grounds and behind enemy lines. God is everywhere.

Reginald G. Johnson, Ph.D

12.

The Awakening

This is the final stage of your being—where you are "aware" and "awake" to your higher sensory perception and spiritual self. You can now assist others to create love, spiritual advancement and power in their lives, creating the force known as...the Awakening.—

Anything people do not understand, they seek to avoid or destroy. This includes paranormal experience, UFOs, the spirit world, or anything outside the physical body and its five senses. Then, there are those souls who, in the face of danger, will say to the mountain, "Be thou removed," and—in spite of all earthbound laws of nature—the mountain is removed. These "mountains" can be physical, emotional, personal, financial, or any kind of obstacle in one's life.

Your own "awakening" arrives at the time of your personal acceptance of it. You must simply realize, as Christ did, that you are spirit first and then you are "who" you are—a birthless, deathless, changeless unit of consciousness animated by God or your own Universal subconscious "self."

s of mind have been documented and throughout time. It has been eye-witnessed, cross- ied and experienced in groups—yet the integrity of "God in man" is still questioned. I have done readings for many years and I am amazed each time during a reading: some client will demonstrate a powerful emotion and cry (as confirmation and release), laugh, squirm in their seats, and gasp in shock at someone's name being called in the session who is unknown to me—and then walk away in doubt! Incredible and true. Many clients who know me always hear this mantra, "Worry is a spiritual sickness and doubt is prayer in reverse." Until you master your thinking, you won't master your destiny. The inner, subconscious mind must accept conscious input and must demonstrate the results in physical reality.

In creating your own awakening, you have to open your mind to its latent powers. Learn to listen to the voice of God within you. Every person must learn to quiet the mind, guard against random thoughts, and for 28 days "declare" that you are what you choose to be and that your place in life and spirit improves because of your impenetrable faith! Prophets, or seers, from centuries past and also presently, are given the gift of prophecy or clairvoyance and are able to "see" future events for themselves, others, a nation, or the world. True modern-day seers are able to detect energies, which some term angels and others call spirits, who have passed on. Love remains with you, no matter if it's in the body or out-of-body. In developing your own psychic abilities, you must "allow" its emanation and development by never forcing it. It's like a relationship between people—you don't "order" or force a relationship; you "nurture" or allow its development with love.

There are a myriad of gifts from God. Some people have the gift of clairaudience, or supernatural hearing; some receive the gift of psychometry (touching objects and sensing the owner of the object and incidents surrounding it); and some are given the gift of telekinesis, or moving objects with the mind. God was good to me. He gave me many of these gifts, which have developed even further with study and practice to help others. Do not overlook "hunches" or "gut feelings" in your prayers and meditations. God came to Moses in a dream; John the Baptist "knew" of the coming Messiah. The Messiah "knew" about his own death and the events surrounding it. You must "know" your gift so that you may assist other souls to grow and develop to their place of "awakening" or enlightenment.

My favorite aspect of the wonderful gifts of God is the one used by mediums (those who communicate with departed souls from this planet). This gift truly confirms love and life beyond the grave—or immortality.

When you forgive others, something incredible happens— you invite the very energy of God and his angels into your life experience. Forgiveness heals hurts on all levels. Go within yourself and enter the sacred space with thanks. You will find that people around you are more loving and supportive and you will view them differently. I am on the spiritual "super highway" when phone calls come in about problems of love, children, separation, finance, death, and other problems, which all stem from spirits not yet enlightened, or awakened.

Forgiveness Exercise: Try this exercise. Take a deep breath through your nose. Hold the breath for the mental count of 5, 4, 3, 2, 1—release the breath slowly through your mouth in a stream of air, relaxing your neck, shoulders, arms, hands, chest and stomach. Repeat this process several times.

Now, "see" yourself in your mind's eye, on this incredible beach with white sand, a beautiful blue, cloudless sky, and the warm sun shining down on you. The water is clear, and there is a school of multi-colored fish swimming and playing together. As you admire all this, you bend down and with your index finger, write the name or names of people you believe you need to forgive or those who should forgive you. After you have clearly written down their names, stand up and see an ocean wave come in and see the names being washed off the beach carrying them into the deep Universal Unconscious where the ego is erased and there is nothing but the eternity of love and forgiveness. Know that you and the name(s) of those you have written in the sand have been forgiven, and vice versa. This is how you venture inward. This is also the technique used in developing altered states of consciousness. You've done this before.

Repeatedly using this and other forms of meditation will activate the opening of the right temporal lobe of the brain—the "God" part, or link with you and the Eternal. You should record this session on tape and replay it for 28 days and notice the shape of your own development and increase in potency. This part of your mind is the area of healing, psychic powers, visions, remote viewing, and your potential to experience union with God. The beach represents freedom and relaxation.

I would tell my clients this all the time: "Your attitude of gratitude will increase your spiritual latitude." When they practiced this attitude in their prayers, rituals and meditation, they experienced more success, prosperity and love.

There is a thin, highly transparent veil between physical and subconscious reality. You can effect a new reconstructive state of being simply by having an open heart and mind. Yes, it takes some discipline to attune to the voice of God for your life. Your conscious mind will have doubts and resistance. But you will approach your sacred time with God with an attitude of thanks and a calm spirit. Remain in the stillness and information will pour through you. After your meditations, you may want to keep a tape recorder or Spirit Journal near you to record the impressions, vibrations, feelings and voices.

Do your meditations (if possible), at the same time to establish the ritual in your subconscious mind, making it easier and easier to "get into the mind set." This is a lifelong journey, not a twitch of the nose, wave of the hand, or a three heel-click kind of spiritual awakening. You must incorporate the practices in your daily living.

I use Tarot cards, psychometry and palm readings for clients. But this came about as the Spirit of God directed me. To be certain God was coming through me in my early meditations and prayer, I would give free readings to friends and relatives. They began telling me the things I told them either were true or later came true. Voila! That was truly a "religious" experience for me. I called on angels that revealed themselves to me in dreams and meditations and it proved incredibly successful for me. The Bible says a true prophet's predictions come true!

In terms of psychometry (which is the art of holding objects and giving the impressions you "feel" from the object), this "just happened" to me. I was holding a photograph and "heard" a car crash and "saw" a motorcycle with a teenager on it. The young woman who handed me the photograph confirmed, in amazement, that everything was true!

Tarot cards are an ancient art of deciphering a formation or pattern of cards randomly drawn from 78 images to gain insight and mastery over issues of relationships, opportunities, and life's events. Tarot's roots go back to antiquity but some scholars believe it originates in 14th Century Italy and France.

You will be "directed" to the cards that are right for you. There are many books of Tarot to study. Allow the Spirit to guide you to the right cards for you.

The experience of "the Awakening" as a paranormal experience is not unusual in the Bible, Koran, Torah or any other inspired religious text on this planet. Nearly all spiritual leaders have "heard the Voice of God." Well, God did not vanish and simply stop speaking.

Regardless of our cultural, tribal or other differences, we cannot afford to maintain bias on any level in this world, including that of our ethnographic dissimilarity. We must use our bridge-building efforts to unconditionally understand each other. This should be a 21st Century "wake up" call to preserve and promote the quality of life on earth.

Our religious tolerance will be the Christ-like trait to help us bear the weight of spiritual traffic on the bridge to the unseen universe of God. To deny any of our human, Christian, Catholic, Jewish or other likenesses will only risk perpetuating the fragmentation of a great spiritual divide among the religions on earth.

Not all psychics want to help people, and unfortunately, neither do all preachers—some have lost contact with God and worship money, overlooking the true spiritual needs and counsel of the seeker. You are the ultimate vehicle of "the Awakening."

There are countless examples of telepathy, clairvoyance, mediumship, out-of-body travel, transfiguration, resurrection (returning from the dead, a Voodoo practice today), levitation (walking on water and ascending into clouds), and other paranormal experiences in the Bible. Jesus even declared, as stated earlier, that we would do the things He did and more! We cannot afford the luxury of judgment or bias in the spiritual walk. We are all linked, although our practices and methods vary. In achieving the Christ Consciousness and the spiritual growth called "the Awakening," we realize that it rains on the "just" and the "unjust" alike. This is a true cosmic paradox in this world. On your road to "the Awakening" you will have an intuitive perception of a cosmic mystery giving your life amazing significance, meaning, and the beauty of spirituality, or holiness. Many Christian churches no longer practice the New Moon Ritual and Sabbaths as did Moses and Solomon. Fortunately, Wiccans have never stopped observing this Jewish ordinance and lost Christian observance. The Bible has at least twenty-four references to the New Moon. The New Moon provides energy shifts and a spiritual "recharge" each month. I practice this ritual, directed by the Holy Spirit. Does your church do this?

There was a reflecting pool in the Bible where an Angel came monthly and "stirred" the waters. The first person to enter the pool during this time would be miraculously healed of any sickness. Where are the Angels hanging out today? Where are the reflecting pools of healing? This is Bible-based information which must be weighed carefully before judging others for their beliefs. I am encouraged in a positive manner when someone asks me, "Why don't they teach this in our church?" Many times it is because we tend to think God only attends a particular church.

Great mystics know that we are infinite beings created by the Infinite God and linked to Him from every part of the Universe by the Indwelling Holy Spirit Who knows all. You may call this female energy Divinity, Goddess, or other aspects of the female energy of God.

As residents of Earth, we need to assist God as Lightworkers to improve the quality of life on earth in its varying forms and species—on all levels and beyond the veil of eternity. God bless you in your search to find "the Awakening."

Reginald G. Johnson, Ph.D

No activity is more fascinating than that of self-transformation.

Reginald G. Johnson, Ph.D

ABOUT THE AUTHOR

Reginald G. Johnson was born in Bishopville, South Carolina, later moving to Washington, D.C. As far back as he can remember, he was always able to "see" things beyond the physical reality of knowing. He has also written newspaper and magazine articles for local and online publications.

He is a teacher and inspirational speaker who has appeared on radio station 97.1 FM (in the company of *The Howard Stern Show*), on 93.1 "Arrow 93" rock station, and is the official psychic for station 103.9 F.M. in San Bernardino, California. In addition, he has appeared on several local television shows. Reggie teaches classes in psychic development, esoteric philosophy, magick, Hermetic Christianity, and Tarot at the Mystery School of the ULC, in Cerritos, California, a school he founded.

For more information, call Toll Free (866) 711-8324. Or write to the author c/o Mystic Visions, 17221 Harvest Avenue, Cerritos, CA 90703.

Printed in the United States
28936LVS00005B/259-306